The Story of
Billy McCarrell

The Story of
Billy McCarrell

DOROTHY MARTIN

LARKSPUR, COLORADO

Grace Acres Press
PO Box 22
Larkspur, CO 80118
www.GraceAcresPress.com

CULTIVATING JOY

This book was first published in the United States by
Moody Publishers, 820 N. LaSalle Blvd., Chicago,
IL 60610 with the title *The Story of Billy McCarrell*,
copyright © 1983 by The Moody Bible Institute of Chicago. Used by
permission. All rights reserved.

All Scripture quotations in this book are from the New American
Standard Bible, © 1960, 1962, 1963, 1968, 1971, 1972, 1973, 1975, and
1977 by the Lockman Foundation, and are used by permission.

Printed in the United States of America.
25 24 23 22 21 20 19   1 2 3 4 5 6

Print ISBN: 978-1-60265-060-2
Ebook ISBN: 978-1-60265-061-9

Library of Congress Cataloging-in-Publication Data:

Table of Contents

Chapter 1

Samuel McCarrell's quick, nervous strides paced him back and forth through the small house on DeKoven Street as he waited for the thin newborn cry that would announce the baby's safe arrival. His thoughts were as abrupt as his movements.

Something could go wrong. Death in childbirth. It happened often among the poor in Chicago. How well he knew! He shut his mind to the hurting memory of his first wife's death, leaving him with a baby daughter and a young son.

He peered out at the dirty snow piled in the streets. Here it was in to the second week in February, and the bitter weather still held on. Icy winds off Lake Michigan rattled the windows and slipped through cracks to frost the windowsills.

Samuel shoved more fuel into the small stove, rubbing his hands nervously in the warmth. He was fortunate to have a job to buy coal to keep the house reasonably warm for Sarah and the children. His friends who had taken part in a strike two years ago had been blacklisted and hadn't worked since. They had no money for fuel — or food.

He shook his head as he remembered the newspaper description he had read of some of Chicago's tenements—frame jungles, the paper had called them. He'd been in one like that last week. Four families squeezed into two tiny rooms with no heat against the winter winds and no windows to let in the sun.

"That's the worst of all," he muttered. "No sun."

He listened at the bedroom door. Why was it taking so long? He turned away, gnawing his lip. He had to think of something to keep his mind occupied. He flipped through the newspaper again—the story of the costume party Marshall Field had given last month for his two children. It had made him so angry his voice had shaken when he read it to Sarah.

The paper had described the yard around the Field mansion, white puffs of snow topping the ornate grillwork on the iron fence surrounding the spacious grounds. The guests had pulled up to the wide front doors in horse-drawn carriages, thick rugs keeping them warm in their Oriental costumes.

Samuel remembered the reporter's exclamations about the high-ceilinged gold and ivory room, and the circular carved staircase. The electric lights—the first to be used in a private home in Chicago, the reporter had said as proudly as though they had been his own—had reflected the silver and crystal on the lavishly spread tables.

"Seventy-five thousand dollars for one party!" Samuel spat the words now in scorn and anger. "Sure, and it's sinful to spend such money for a party when children in this city search garbage cans for a crust to gnaw on."

He knew men like Field and Pullman and Armour claimed it was no one else's business what they did with their money. It was theirs, earned by hard work and long hours. They had started poor and worked their way up. Anyone could do the same, they claimed. If a man was poor, it was proof he was lazy. Samuel knew even some ministers were preaching that.

"I'm not lazy." Samuel heard himself growling the words out loud. "I'll do anything — sell potatoes on the street corner if I have to. But I'll still never be rich."

He stopped pacing to look around the room. When people found that he lived on DeKoven Street, someone always gave a knowing wink and a sly laugh and said, "Right where the big fire started, eh? Was it your cow kicked over the lantern?"

He used to let his fiery temper lash out at the half-sneering question. Now he simply shrugged it off, didn't even try to explain that the fire had happened ten years before he had emigrated from Ireland and that his house was a good three blocks from the O'Leary barn.

The thin wail from the bedroom checked his pacing. The baby! Was Sarah all right? He burst through the door, ignoring the doctor, and strode to the bed, sinking down on his knees. Sarah lay contentedly, the tiny, red-haired baby secure in the curve of her arm.

She looked up at him with wonder in her eyes.

"A boy, Samuel. Little William is finally here. Isn't he beautiful?"

He dragged a chair to the side of the bed and sat down, reaching to fold the blanket back from the little red face. "Our first, Sarah."

She nodded, her eyes misting with tears. Her voice trembled as she whispered, "William is *our* first, Samuel, yes. But he's really our third. I never will make a difference between our children and the two oldest."

Samuel reached to grip her hand, his voice too choked to speak. Then he looked down at the tiny bundle. "What a cold day to be born — February 8, 1886. I wonder — will anyone but us remember? Will he *be* someone?"

"Why, Samuel McCarrell! Of course he will be someone," Sarah retorted. Then her laugh came low and warm. "Likely every new parent thinks his child will change the world."

Sarah stayed in bed the next few days with Samuel coming to sit beside her as often as possible. He looked down at the baby. "I wonder what's in store for this little one. Glad I am that he was born in this country. Hard as times are here, they are worse where we came from, Sarah."

She nodded, her eyes shadowed with memories. "Before I signed to come when my brother needed a housekeeper, I heard fearful stores of the ships that carried immigrants. Coffin ships, they said, with death a passenger. With people packed so close below decks, sickness spread like wind."

"I too heard stories of the ships." Samuel nodded. "I didn't know if I was right to leave my little town of Armagh for this unknown country. But then I thought, how could the unknown be worse than what we were enduring? The potato famine left us with nothing. Children cried in the streets. And the Catholic-Protestant fighting—" He stopped, a scowl darkening his face.

Sarah reached to hold his hand. "When my brother went back to Ireland after I came all the way across the ocean to keep house for him, it was the thought of those terrible waves that kept me here—"

"Sure, and I thought it was my handsome face that made you stay," Samuel teased.

"That some," she admitted, smiling at the Irish lilt of his voice.

"And now I have plans." Samuel leaned back, crossing his legs, thumbs hooked in his belt. "I don't expect ever to be a millionaire, but I do intend to provide well for you and the children. If God helps those who help themselves, as they say, then we'll get along. We'll not remain here forever, Sarah, where we are easy prey for the politicians who buy our votes with the promise of food and jobs."

"You've never gotten your jobs that way!"

"No, but we Irish have the advantage of knowing English, so we can stick up for our rights. The poor folks from Poland and Germany and Italy and Hungary don't understand what's being said to them, don't know when someone cheats them. They get charged ten cents for a hunk of sausage that's not worth two cents. I've gotten my head bashed more than once for sticking up for some poor fellow being cheated. What makes my blood boil is that some of the immigrants were high-class people in their old countries — professors and lawyers. Here, because they can't speak English, they can only get jobs sweeping streets and cleaning sewers. And they've got to sell their souls for that."

Sarah reached a hand in protest. "Sam! Don't get yourself so worked up. You can't take on everyone's troubles."

"You've got to speak up when you see things happening that aren't right, even if you get a black eye for your pains."

He reached for the newspaper, stuck as usual in his back pocket. "I tell you, Sarah, this city is in a mess, and it's getting worse every day, every election. Listen to this editorial. Whoever wrote it knows what's going on. It says,

> "Chicago is the Nineveh of political corruption and the Sodom and Gomorrah of moral corruption. Everything and anything is for sale on the streets of Chicago, from a political job to a girl's innocence. Civic and business leaders pay for favors from political bosses. No one dares resist for fear

of finding his business in flames or himself maimed or threatened with death. City Council members are known as Gray Wolves for their voracious corruption."

He crumpled the newspaper in his fist, and his voice hard with anger and fear. "Sarah, working men are so desperate that they listen to anyone who promises a way out — even those who talk of overthrowing the government. If some of those big money men don't yield to the demands of the laboring class, there's going to be trouble. In this city and in the whole country."

He sat brooding while Sarah watched him anxiously. She ran a gentle hand over the soft red fuzz on the baby's head. "I wonder if this little one has inherited your fire."

"I hope so," Samuel rumbled, his mind still worrying about the problems. "What was it that fellow said? I read it someplace. Something about how the poor are needed so the rich can practice their Christian charity —"

Sarah's laugh bubbled. "Samuel, if everyone read as much as you do, they'd have no time for trouble. Do pass your love of books on to this little one to keep him out of mischief."

The harsh winter gradually warmed into spring, and Samuel's fears over labor unrest grew. He shook his head over the death of a striker in a skirmish with police during a long strike at the McCormick works.

"There'll be trouble," he warned as he read the newspapers and listened to men talk. He sensed that the attitude of the middle-class people in the city was shifting from sympathy for the working man to fear of trouble and anarchy. Letters to the newspapers increasingly criticized men who threatened to strike for an eight-hour day. Others showed anxiety at the small group of agitators who openly advocated overthrowing the government.

"Can't people see that a man gets desperate when he works twelve to fifteen hours a day for wages that won't buy a sack of potatoes?" Samuel fumed.

He continually warned Sarah against taking the children out on the streets. "Even in the daytime it isn't safe."

Sarah pushed her hair back from her forehead in a weary gesture. "When we get these hot, muggy days, I sometimes long for the cool, clear days of Ireland."

Samuel laughed. "Just remember how cold it was in February when the baby came. But I agree. Here it is the first of May, and the summer's heat is already here."

His voice was serious as he went on. "It's not just the weather that's hot. Tempers are, too. People are in an ugly mood. The strikes taking place all across the country have stirred up a lot of wild talking and writing. Some of it is justified, but some of it is just plain wrong. All this talk about making the people the government. That's what democracy *is*, even if it doesn't always work just right. Stay close to home, Sarah. It wouldn't take much to set off real trouble, and I don't want you caught in it."

His predictions came true a few days later. He stumbled home to tell Sarah about it, his face ashen.

"It just—just—burst out. A crowd was gathered in Haymarket Square—they'd been milling around for a time. Someone said a thousand or more were jammed together listening to speeches. Police were everywhere, watching for trouble. The mayor even rode around on his horse, joking some with people, and then urged them to go home. It started to drizzle, and people were ducking for shelter when suddenly someone threw something—a bomb, they said. People screamed and ran every which way. Some policemen were hurt, and they began shooting. I'm glad I wasn't there. I don't know the truth of it all—who's to blame. The reports I heard are wild. But there'll be hangings, I fear."

"Oh, Samuel, can't we move somewhere? Can't we get away from all the trouble? Away from the saloons and gambling houses? I'm afraid even to walk out. The dirty streets and the gamblers and—and the women—trying to lure men—" She stopped, blushing to speak of it, even to her husband.

He shook he head. "Sarah, there's no place we can get away from drink and gambling and all that goes with it. There's not a place like that in all this world."

"But if we could just move from this crowded part of Chicago to someplace where the children could have more freedom."

"We will. I promise, Sarah."

Samuel read the newspapers carefully and listened to the bitter talk of out-of-work men. He watched helplessly as depression swept toward Chicago from the western states. He saw the increasing hostility to the waves of immigrants fleeing oppression in other countries. And he listened to Sarah's pleas that somehow they must leave the dangerous city.

In 1891, when Billy was five, Samuel finally moved his family to the wide prairie at the west edge of the city. They were one of the first families to settle in Harlem, later called Forest Park, one mile from the Harlem Racetrack.

Sarah soon discovered that Chicago was not the only place with vice and crime and corruption. Evil flourished in Harlem also, with the race track so close. As her children grew, she felt threatened for them, the two oldest and her own three sons, Billy, Samuel, and John.

"But we're not as bad off as the poor in the city," Samuel reminded her. "The mayor wanted the World's Fair held in Chicago because he thought it would bring prosperity, or at least lift the depression. Instead, hundreds of poor people are homeless. A lot of them sleep nights on the stairs in City Hall and eat from garbage cans. I suppose the city should get some credit for giving some help to the jobless. The paper says the city pays men ten cents an hour to clean the streets. They spread the work around by letting the single men work only three hours a day. Married men with families can work eight hours."

Sarah shuddered and looked at the fragrant bread she had just taken from the oven. "And I thought *we* were hit by the depression." She sighed then and held up a pair of Billy's pants. "I declare, that boy is never going to stop growing—out as much as up."

"He is shooting up," Samuel agreed, his voice proud. "Eight years old already."

"Samuel, I'm worried about him. He's not running with a good group of boys." She broke off, anxiety jabbing the needle around the patch on Billy's pants. "It riles me when the papers talk about this part of town being—being—"

"Little Hell?"

"Yes. The papers say it has the most saloons and gambling houses and—and other places of any town in Illinois. They sound proud of the description. And it makes the boys, even the young ones, think they have to live up to the reputation. And Billy follows right along. In fact, he is the ringleader of the boys his age."

"He's just a boy, Sarah. Mischievous, yes. I know he loves practical jokes, and maybe sometimes they do get out of hand—"

"And he's using bad language," Sarah broke in indignantly, "especially when he gets mad about something. He *must* learn to control his temper, Samuel."

"I'll get after him for that. The temper goes with the red hair, I suppose."

"He can't do anything about his hair, but he certainly can learn to control his tongue," Sarah retorted.

Samuel did get after Billy in the next few years. He and his younger brothers listened, but they liked the nickname they and their friends had acquired.

"Don't let Ma know we're called Little Hell's bums," Billy warned his brothers.

If his parents didn't know his reputation, the neighbors and schoolteachers did. So did the Sunday school teachers at Pioneer Chapel, a branch of the First Presbyterian Church of Oak Park. Samuel insisted that the family go to church regularly. He was proud of his knowledge of the Bible and taught a Sunday school class.

Samuel worked hard to keep the promise he had made Sarah when Billy was born. He worked as a wood finisher of Pullman cars, and, by careful, shrewd managing, saved enough money to buy a book business. He moved his family into a decent neighborhood in Oak Park. By the time Billy graduated from the eighth grade in 1900, Samuel was a dealer in exclusive books and fine prints, going to his office in Chicago every day.

Billy was restless after finishing school, craving action. One day he announced, "I'm going to business college. I can take a seven-month stenographic course and then get a good job and make money."

"Fine," Samuel answered. "I can use you in the business when you finish. I'll be glad of your company on the El ride. Maybe later I'll change the name of the business to S. J. McCarrell and Son, Publishers."

"I'm willing to work all week as long as I have time for Sunday football," Billy answered.

Sarah turned to face him, hands on hips. "It worries me that you play that rough game. The papers call it the most brutal and violent sport—" She stopped to shake her head. "Though why it is called a sport, I'll never understand. You don't wear anything to protect your head."

"Ma! You want me to be a sissy?"

"Someday you'll get a serious head injury."

"Don't worry about me, Ma. I always give the other guy more than he gives me. Anyway, broken bones are worth it if we win. And we always do. We're the champs."

"That's because you knock everyone out when you're quarterbacking," John said. "I'd hate to play opposite you."

··•●•··

"Hey, Bill, how long are you gonna keep going to church?" a football friend demanded one Sunday afternoon.

"As long as there's any fun there."

"Fun?"

"Sure. I can keep the teachers going around in circles better than anyone."

Billy went to church on Sunday, January 14, 1904, mentally going over plays for the afternoon game. Suddenly he heard the minster say, "There they crucified Him."

The words jolted him, striking him with a picture of what Jesus Christ had done for him. *He died for me!* The words repeated themselves in his mind. He closed his eyes in silent prayer.

God, You have saved my soul. I want You now to have as much of my life as the devil had before.

He knew that meant all of him. When he got home, he wrote down his feelings to remind himself of the wonder of what had happened to him. "At the age of eighteen... possessing a mean temper and a filthy tongue, I received Jesus Christ as my Savior. He did wondrous things for me."

His inner life changed immediately, but the outward transformation took longer. Other people watched and prayed for him. A year after he was saved, he pulled a birthday card from the mail from a Sunday school teacher who had almost given up hope that Billy McCarrell would ever change. Her desire to encourage him was clear in the greeting.

> We thank God for your young life and all its promise for the future of help and strength for those who are weaker. It is not of your inward life that I am anxious, but that in this coming year you will strive to make your outer life a fit setting for the

soul within. Strive to attain more in the things of which the world will judge you, but, of course, not to the detriment of your spiritual life. A leader of men must, by his outward appearance as well as the hidden powers within, inspire those whom he would lead.

Billy frowned over the words, not sure just what she meant, but resenting the advice. He already had his bad language under control Curses no longer poured out, even when his temper flared. What did she mean by this outward appearance? Since he lived at home, his mother saw that his clothes were clean. He tried to keep his red hair slicked down and his fingernails clean.

"Maybe she's talking about my grammar," he muttered. "If English were as interesting as history, I could have gotten A's in that, too. But I guess I can still improve."

He had already changed another habit. At his first football game after he was saved, he said, "Hey, let's play on Saturday from now on."

"How come? We've always played on Sundays. We don't want to change." The protests shouted him down.

He shrugged. "OK. But you'll have to get someone in my place."

"You can't quit. We need you if we're gonna win."

"I'm too busy on Sunday. After church I'm going to a mission in Chicago to teach a class."

"Hey, fellows. Billy's got religion—" The player

backed away as Billy advanced on him, fists cocked. "OK, change the game to Saturday, then."

As Billy studied and taught, he discovered how much he didn't know about the Bible. He needed training.

Riding the El to work one day, he broached the subject to his father. "I need some training in the Bible."

"Well, I can help you. I've got some books —"

"No, I mean real study. In school."

"Billy, you've worked into the business so well I'd sure hate to lose you. You're such a good talker that you're one of my best salesmen."

"Either Sam or John could take over what I'm doing. I'm really serious about this, Dad. Here I am almost twenty-four, and I don't know what God wants to do with my life. I've got to know more about the Bible."

"Where would you go?"

"To Moody Bible Institute up on LaSalle and Chicago. It only costs three fifty a week for room and board. Plus an hour of work each day. And it'll only take me two years. By the time I finish, maybe I'll know what God wants me to do."

···•••···

As Billy walked into his dingy dorm room, a rat scurried across the floor. He wondered what he was doing in this situation, when a comfortable room awaited him at home. But, setting his bags down, he fell to his knees in the middle of the floor.

"I will live on bread and water, and I'll sleep on the floor, if You will give me the ability through Your Holy Spirit to make Your Word clear to the people I will minister to." After a moment, he began to unpack.

Billy's collar felt too tight and his suit too heavy for the warmth of the room as he walked into his first class in the spring term of 1910. The wide doors of the building stood open to April's unusual warmth. Fans whirred overhead in the big lecture room where students crowded close together on straight chairs—men on one side of the room, and women on the other.

Billy thought of the ten years he had been out of school and the time he had wasted when he had been in school. What if he found the work too hard? What if everyone else was smarter than he? He looked around at the other students and began to relax. Some of them, older than he, looked as anxious as he felt.

He settled back, Bible and notebook and pen ready, as Dr. James M. Gray, president of the school, began to lecture. Billy forgot his surroundings, forgot that others breathed near him as he listened to the clear, quiet voice.

"If you want to know what the Bible says, you must read it. If you expect to master the Bible, you must read it again and again and again. Begin at the beginning and read it continuously and repeatedly. Punctuate the reading of it with prayer to its divine author for understanding. Only in this way will God's Word open to you."

Billy sat motionless when the class ended, overwhelmed by all he had heard. He remembered the Institute's objectives in the catalog: To train men and women in the knowledge of the English Bible, gospel music, personal evangelism, and practical methods of Christian work, emphasis being laid upon the developing and deepening of the spiritual life.

He nodded his head. He had come to the right place. The Bible was central here. He felt at home.

He plunged into his studies with the same enthusiasm he had given to football. But the studies he most enjoyed were his practical Christian work assignments. He liked riding out in the Institute's horse-drawn carriages to hold street meetings and children's Bible classes. He practiced sermons in missions, talking in a loud voice to cover shuffling feet and loud whispers that wondered when the preaching would be finished and the soup served. He learned how to give the gospel in simple sentences to men in jail and to those dying in hospitals. He felt a special sympathy for the drink-soaked derelicts who staggered Chicago's refuse-littered streets.

But his most important assignment was at Pioneer Chapel, where he had accepted Christ and committed himself to Him. He became the Sunday school superintendent and loved the work. It was a school assignment, but it was more than an assignment. His heart beat faster each Sunday, anticipating seeing slender, dark-eyed Minnie Mense.

He had noticed her several years earlier at church activities, and he liked both her quietness and the sparkle of her dark eyes. While still working for his father, he had discovered that she too rode the El from Oak Park to a job in Chicago.

"Where do you get on the El in the city?" he casually asked.

"At the Laflin station."

Later that week, Minnie looked around as someone spoke her name. "Oh, hello," she answered, surprise clear in her voice.

Billy lifted his hat. "I, uh — I — how are you? I'm — I'm riding to Oak Park, too."

It was several weeks before Minnie discovered that Billy took the El from downtown as far as her station. Then he got off to wait until she came so he could ride the rest of the way with her.

The first time he got up enough nerve to ask her for a date was with an invitation to hear William Newell preach. They also went to hear Billy Sunday and sat fascinated by his pulpit antics.

"Is all that jumping around and yelling good?" Minnie asked.

"Maybe not *that* much moving around. But you do have to talk loud enough so people will hear you. You have to let people know you mean what you say."

Minnie's mother began to question the frequency of Billy's name and opinions in Minnie's conversation. Minnie told Billy about it just before his graduation from Moody.

"What did you tell her about us?"

"That we're keeping steady company. But that you aren't sure what you will do when you finish school."

She didn't tell him her mother's next question. "What does he want to do? He should know by now. After all, he's twenty-six."

"Mother, he just wants to be a witness for God."

"That doesn't bring in money to live on. He'll need a church."

"He isn't interested in making money. He believes God will provide. And he's so—so energetic. He doesn't like things to come too easily. When he graduates, he'll have offers from churches."

Billy knew Minnie's confidence about his future. He saw her sitting proudly in the audience when he graduated in April, 1912, listening intently as he represented the seniors as class speaker. He knew she was proud of the description of him in the yearbook— "a sweet spirit and a strong will."

Even after his graduation, marriage was not immediate. Billy didn't ask her to be his wife, though his intentions showed in his eyes when he looked at her.

He told her about the offers he had from several churches. But none of them seemed to him to come from the Lord. He had a hard time explaining his hesitation to people who asked, "What are you waiting for? You've got the training. Why aren't you using it?"

Only Minnie shared his inner burden and gave understanding. She listened as he talked. "I look around and see some of the fellows I grew up with, the ones I played ball with every week. Some of them are gamblers; others are just bums staggering around on Skid Row. Some are in jail."

He stopped to shake his head and finish soberly. "I'd be one of them if God hadn't saved me. I owe Him my life. I tell you, Minnie, I *know* that when God enters your soul, He changes your personality and your life."

He heard the longing in Minnie's voice as she said, "If you were to take a church — like one of those you've been offered — then you could see if it is the place God wants you to be."

Clear in her voice was the underlying meaning, "Then we could be married."

Billy stood up, looking away from the hope in her eyes. "Minnie, I've got to tell you. That church in Canada, the one that's been after me to come as the minister — well — Minnie, I've made up my mind not to take it."

He still couldn't look at her, didn't want to see the hope fade from her face. Then he turned impulsively. "Minnie, I can't tell this to anyone but you. But I've told God that I would take the hardest place in America, no matter what the sacrifice to me, personally."

He stopped, looking at her, pleading for her understanding. "Even if it means giving you up, I want to do what God wants."

Chapter 2

"William, did you carry home the library's entire history section?" Sarah looked affectionately at her son.

Billy looked up from the pile of books long enough to smile at her and then went back to his reading. His studies at Moody Bible Institute had opened a new world of biblical study, and he read voraciously. But the books also discussed the views of higher criticism, and the more he read, the angrier he got. To think that ministers and seminary professors were teaching that the Bible was not inspired by God, but was a human document; that the miracles in Scripture were "poetic fancies"; that the Pentateuch was not written by Moses under God's direction but was a maze of sources; that the book of Daniel was not a prophecy but was written after the events had happened.

Accompanying this swing away from belief in Scripture were the notions of the social gospel, which deemphasized the need for individual, personal salvation. He plowed through Walter Rauschenbusch's newly published *Christianity in the Social Order*, muttering snatches aloud. "Sins of society must be attacked…eliminate poverty and injustice and man will reach his highest good … man is a product of his environment."

"Rubbish! The change has got to be inward in order to be lasting. How well I know that."

He turned with relief to the *Fundamentals* booklets, recognizing names of writers like Dr. Gray and Dr. Torrey who knew the truth. They wrote clearly and precisely, stating the facts of the inspiration of Scripture, Christ's virgin birth, His atoning sacrifice, His resurrection, ascension, and second coming. As he read, Billy recognized what Dr. Gray meant when he had insisted in class that Christians must exhibit good scholarship in order for the worldly educated to listen with respect.

The words echoed in his ears. "Use accurate English; write clearly; be firm but courteous." He checked his notes from one of Dr. Gray's classes, nodding in agreement at the words he had copied.

"Higher criticism *itself* is a legitimate approach to the study of Scripture. We must know the *who* as well as the *what* of our faith. But we reject the higher critical conclusion that Scripture is a human document. The doctrine of inspiration is the dividing line between orthodox and liberal theology.

Billy read and thought and prayed and shared with Minnie what he was learning and the conclusions he was reaching.

"Listen to this," he said one day early in 1913, shaking out the newspaper in imitation of his father.

"Listen to this editorial."

> Like a tapestry where the design of the colors and threads of the upper side blend into a beautiful picture, so Chicago looks to visitors who see only the elegant homes, the silk and satin gowns of society, the lavish display in expensive hotels and mansions.

> But the underside of Chicago, like the knotted and clipped threads of the back side of the tapestry, is a maze of unsafe streets, sweatshops, child labor, disease, rank smells, sordid dens of vice, and rat and vermin-infested shacks so crowded with people that love and tenderness cannot survive the unending struggle just to exist.

"Oh, Bill, I've seen some of those places." Minnie's eyes were shadowed, remembering horrifying sights. "Going into Chicago, the El passes close to some of them. Those poor people — the way they live — the garbage piled in the streets — the enormous rats that dart in and out —"

"But the worst of it is that they don't have hope in the Lord," Billy burst out. "Trusting Him at least gives hope for a future life. Oh, I go along with the need for social justice. No one should live so wretchedly. But above everything else the greatest need anyone has is to know Jesus Christ as Savior. That's the message I want to preach."

Minnie looked at him shyly. "Then, maybe, somewhere around here is the place you want? The hard place you are looking for?"

He nodded soberly. "I think so. I'm sure God will show me that place very soon." He opened his Bible. "Minnie, I've chosen John fifteen sixteen as my life verse:

> "Ye have not chosen me, but I have chosen you, and ordained you that ye should go and bring forth fruit, and that your fruit should remain: that whatsoever ye shall ask of the Father in my name, he may give it you."

"I'm going to take that as God's promise to me personally in whatever hard place He puts me."

He bounced in one day with news. "Minnie! I've been asked to preach at a Congregational church in Cicero over on Fifty-second Avenue and Twenty-fourth Street. I'm told it's small and not many people attend."

"Cicero? That's where the Western Electric Telephone Company is, isn't it? Isn't that a strong Czech community? Won't a lot of people be Catholic?"

"I suppose so. Anyway, I'm to preach morning and evening on June Fourth."

"I wish I could go with you, but I don't think I can find anyone to take my class at the chapel."

William went eagerly that June Sunday, getting off the streetcar at the corner. His steps slowed as he approached the building and stopped where the sidewalk ended. He swallowed hard at the sight facing him. His eyes followed a weed-overgrown path to a paint-bare building with loose, weather-beaten shingles. The sagging front door stood open to the hot June sun. Billy fanned himself with his hat as he slowly walked to the entrance, stepped inside, and looked around at the room's gray dinginess. Plaster littered the floor behind the pulpit. Sunlight glimmered through open places where the wall's crumbling plaster showed the lathes. Flies droned listlessly against the grimy windows.

The sound of footsteps on the bare floor swung Billy around to face two men.

"You must be Mr. McCarrell." The man's voice was a question as he held his hand out in greeting.

"Yes. I wanted to be sure to be on time for the service."

"I am James Leigh. This is Lambert Klunder. We're glad to have you preach for us today." He cleared his throat, glancing nervously at William. "We—we probably will not have many in the service today. It's summer, you know, vacations cut in—" His voice trailed off into uncertainty.

William laughed. "I don't mind small congregations. I'm just a beginner myself, you see. Tell me something about the church."

He saw the two men glance at one another. "Well, uh—we're a small group at best. That in itself makes some folks discouraged so they don't come regularly." Mr. Leigh stopped to give an embarrassed laugh. "In fact, I must confess that the chairman of the board of deacons is even suggesting that we sell the property—"

"I don't think he was serious," the other man interrupted. "But we, that is, Mr. Leigh and I feel strongly that the children at least need instruction in the Bible. We would hate to see the church close down completely. The problem is our minister isn't— that is, we don't—"

William saw the faint warning headshake Mr. Leigh gave, and Mr. Klunder stopped, staring down at the dirty floor.

"Here comes my wife. Let me introduce you." Mr. Leigh's voice showed his relief that the conversation could end.

Billy counted twenty-five in the congregation, including the half dozen children who spilled in from Sunday school just before he began the service. He led the singing, trying to put into practice the principles of conducting he had learned in music class at Moody. He sang loudly himself to swell the feeble sound.

As Billy read the Scripture and prayed and preached, he felt the intense scrutiny of the two men. At the close of the evening service, Mr. Klunder pressed a five dollar bill into William's hand with an apologetic, "We're sorry it isn't more."

"Doesn't matter. I came for the Lord's sake, not the money."

Again the two men exchanged glances before Mr.

Leigh stepped closer, asking hesitantly, "I don't suppose you'd be willing to come back next Sunday?"

"If you want me, yes," Billy answered, not even trying to keep the eagerness from his voice.

At the close of the next Sunday, Mr. Leigh asked if he would preach for the rest of June. "We like you. We like your style. We'd be obliged if you would just keep a loving eye on this place."

"I will, if you will understand that I will never preach anything but the Word of God."

"That's all we want," Mr. Klunder answered, gripping Billy's hand.

Billy faced Mr. Leigh. "Since I'll be coming back several Sundays, it would help if I knew more about the church."

He waited, and then as the two men hesitated, looking uncomfortable, he tried to put them at ease. "I've noticed you don't seem to want to talk about the situation here. Your regular minister—he's on vacation?"

The direct question broke through their reserve, and they poured out the story of the church and their deep concern for it. Billy listened intently as they told of its beginning in 1892 as a mission work meeting in the Morton Park School House. Then it became the Morton Park Congregational Church, and services were conducted by ministers who came, served briefly, and moved on to better paying positions.

"In 1903 we managed to put up this little frame

building." Mr. Leigh gestured around the battered room. "But then folks just got tired of the struggle and a lot of them quit coming. There's just a handful of us left now and no money to keep the building in shape."

Billy looked around at the grime-smudged plaster of the paintless walls.

"The denomination holds the mortgage on the property, but we're supposed to pay the insurance," Mr. Klunder went on with the explanation. "Of course the property isn't worth much. There's just this little auditorium. Downstairs is the heating plant, a tiny kitchen, and one small Sunday school room."

"We couldn't raise money for the insurance payment when it last came due. And even though the denomination gave twenty-five dollars a month toward the minster's salary, we couldn't raise the rest. In fact, we still owe him back salary even though he's gone." Mr. Leigh finished the dismal recital, his voice gloomy.

The men looked at William, expecting him to turn away in disgust. Instead he said, "Great! I'll be back next Sunday."

"We can't promise more than five dollars a week—"

"That's all right. I'm not married, and my needs are simple." Billy started out the door, but stopped to look back at the men. "Oh. One thing I'd like to ask of you. Please don't ask the denomination to contribute anything toward what you pay me."

He shook hands and went out to wait for the streetcar, eager to tell Minnie the good news. He had a church!

Maybe for the whole summer.

The two men lingered in the doorway, watching the quick, vigorous stride of the young, redheaded preacher.

"Do you suppose—?" They asked the question in unison, and then laughed at the ridiculous expression of hope on each other's face.

Billy came back each Sunday through July and August. He left the door open for air on hot Sundays, even thought the clanging streetcar bells punctuated his sermons. By fall enough people were coming and giving regularly that he received ten dollars a week. He saw the potential in the handful of people when no one else did. He surveyed the community and found that his church, feeble as it was, was the strongest Protestant work in the predominantly Catholic town. Many in the town were free thinkers, indifferent to religion of any kind.

He visited one of the original members of the church and listened to him reminisce.

"We was one of the first families to move here. Seemed like the end of nowhere—just a few shacks straggling 'cross the prairie. We sure felt the wind whippin' across them fields. When folks settled some and houses got bunched together, they got a post office and a name. Guess the name Cicero always did take us all in, but it wasn't much used. This was always Morton Park. That is, till the Western Electric came in. Then all the little places got took in as Cicero."

"How many nationalities are there?"

"Oh, every kind you kin name. Dutch, Irish, Italians. Mostly Czech, we're workers. We don't hold much with gettin' free handouts. Me and my family ain't never taken charity. Don't aim to."

"What about all the liquor and gambling? Not just here, but all around us."

The old man's eyes swam with tears, and his voice quavered. "A lot of us forgot about religion when we come from the old country. Didn't want any. We was sick of the church tellin' us what to do. Trouble is, when we turned from the church we turned from the Lord, too. Me, I was lucky. Some fellow got hold of me and told me I was a sinner. Got me to church. Now you've come, and we're learnin' the Bible. Sure like it."

Billy enjoyed the pastries and coffee the man's wife served and then went home sobered by what he had heard. He stopped to tell Minnie about it.

"I'm not quitting here without putting up a fight. Think of all the time and energy I wasted on football and practical jokes before I was saved. I'm going to use my energy to build that little church."

He leaned over the pulpit desk the next Sunday morning, his voice earnest. "I'm going to promise you something. I will stick with you even if we have to meet in a chicken coop, if you folks understand that while I am here, there will be nothing preached but God's Word. We want a strong church that will be a salting influence to offset the evil around us."

He looked around at the sparse congregation, his voice confident. "We can be an army of warriors for God."

The people looked at him and then at one another. They wanted to believe him, but hardly dared to. Twenty-five people in a morning service, in an unpainted building with no facilities — the preacher and a handful of others at the midweek service — could *they* become an army?

But William had a secret weapon, one he confided to Minnie, who was praying with him about the church. His study in the book of Acts had convinced him that any church would grow if it followed the methods of the early church. Those methods were much prayer, a strong Bible preaching ministry, an evangelistic program to reach the community, and a vigorous missionary outreach. The place for him to practice Acts 1:8 was Cicero, *his* Jerusalem.

Mr. Leigh and Mr. Klunder watched him come eagerly each week. "He's our last hope of saving this church," they agreed, and watched, scarcely daring to believe as they saw the flickering life of the church gradually steady and burn brighter.

The summer of 1913 ended, and the work went on. Billy's energy multiplied as the prairies around Cicero blazed with the reds and golds of autumn and then were buried in deep snow. He preached twice each Sunday and began a young people's group, an adult Sunday school class, and a Friday evening Bible study. With all this activity, he was still not the official minister of the church, but only the Sunday preacher, now with a ten dollar weekly gift.

It was not much to offer a young woman, but William proposed marriage in November 1913. Minnie accepted, not worrying about money as long as she had him.

"We can't get married right away though," he warned. "We don't have enough to set up housekeeping. I just want to be sure you know that you belong to me."

"*I've* known that for a long time," she answered, her smile shy but her eyes sparkling.

Billy's vigorous preaching deepened the life of the members. In turn, they reached out to bring in more people and gave regularly out of skimpy salaries. In January, 1914, they asked him to be their minister at a monthly salary of seventy-five dollars.

People who were not members saw that great things were happening within the walls of the frame building at Fifty-second and Twenty-fourth. The men slapped white paint over the weatherbeaten gray building. They installed ventilators, cleaned the windows, and put up screens. They dug out the weeds at the rear of the building and planted a lawn, fencing it to keep it from being a shortcut to the streetcar line.

The church progressed in other ways than in numbers and finances; the youth group and the Sunday school classes grabbed hold of Acts 1:8, too. They helped support a missionary at the local county poorhouse, collected money and clothes for needy families, and gave money for a national pastor in Korea and two missionaries in Africa.

Sometimes the inside of the church spilled over to the outside. During the summer of 1914, Billy decided to move the Sunday evening service out to the front lawn. The curious who drifted by and stopped to listen were given hymnbooks and invited to join the singing.

The passing streetcars often drowned out Billy's words with their screeching wheels and clanging bells. But each time the streetcar clattered to a stop, Billy seized the moment, even in the middle of his sermon, to bellow out the words of John 3:16. That way he made sure that everyone on the streetcar heard the wonderful message of God's gift of Christ.

Inevitably, people laughed, and some exclaimed, "That Billy McCarrell is nuts."

But looking around Cicero — and Chicago — and the world, William saw ugliness and emptiness and despair. "I'm willing to stand with the apostle Paul as a fool for Christ," he declared.

A crisis mushroomed unexpectedly that summer of 1914, a crisis that grew out of romance. Billy knew all about romance; he was head over heels in love with Minnie and looking forward to their marriage in the fall.

Several couples in the church became engaged and came to him to talk over plans and set a wedding date.

"I'm delighted that you have found the right mates,"

he exclaimed. "I'll gladly give you counsel and show you God's ideal of marriage in Scripture. But I'm sorry, I can't perform your marriage ceremony."

"We don't want anyone but you to do it," one girl protested in tears. "You're the one who brought us to Christ, and we want you to start our life together."

"The problem is that I am not an ordained minister. State laws require that a man be ordained in order to perform weddings. Of course, you could go to the justice of the peace. Or to the minster of another church since I'm sure you want to be married in God's house."

"But you're a Moody graduate. Doesn't that mean you are ordained?"

Billy shook his head. "Moody does not have official sanction to ordain its graduates. Ordination is usually done by the denomination a church belongs to. For us that is the Congregational."

One of the young men smiled his relief. "Oh, well. There's no problem then. Just ask them to do it. But be sure they ordain you before the date we've set for our wedding."

Billy knew the importance of going through proper channels. So his church board made a formal request to headquarters for the ordination of their young energetic pastor. The reply came back that, yes, the denomination would be glad to ordain William McCarrell. They knew he was an effective, able minister because the church had grown more in the few months under his care than in all its previous history.

However, the reply carefully went on to say that the denomination naturally had certain high standards it must maintain.

"We understand that Mr. McCarrell has no formal academic training, particularly seminary training. Moody Bible Institute training is all right as far as it goes. But, of course, it does not equal seminary training. Naturally our Congregational minsters must be well educated to be effective in the pulpit. They require training in more than just the Bible. If Mr. McCarrell will study in one of our seminaries, we will be glad to ordain him upon his graduation."

"I can't agree to that," Billy told his board. "The Congregational seminaries no longer teach certain doctrines that are clearly stated in Scripture. Students are taught in the methods of higher criticism, and they come out saying that the Bible has mistakes in it."

"Well, that won't bother you any," one of the men answered confidently. "You already know what you believe." He gestured around at the other men. "We're not afraid that you'll be swept away by false teaching."

"That's not what's bothering me," Billy answered, hunting for words to express how strongly he felt. "You see, I don't want anyone to think that I agree in the slightest with what they teach. And if I go there and graduate, it will look as though I did agree. And then some other young man who docsn't have as strong convictions as I do might attend and be swept away. I'd be setting a bad example. And you men know what

God says about that in His Word."

Billy asked his people to pray for him in the days of uncertainty that followed. He knew he had to be ordained in order to carry out his full responsibilities as a minister to his people.

"But I can't go just to get an ordination certificate. I simply cannot identify myself with people who doubt God's Word," he insisted to Minnie and to everyone else.

Then God took over. Ministers of other Congregational churches in the Chicago area agreed with William's stand. Many of them were worried by the denomination's drift from belief in the Bible as God's inspired Word. They formed a council and asked Charles Blanchard, president of Wheaton College, to be the chairman. The men asked careful questions of Billy about his knowledge of the Bible and doctrine and his personal commitment to Christ. Satisfied with his answers, they unanimously ordained him to the Christian ministry for the work he had been doing ever since graduating from Moody Bible Institute.

Billy and Minnie and most Americans, busy with the routine of daily living, were only dimly aware of the disastrous political events brewing in Europe. In June a man few Americans knew existed was assassinated in a European town. It seemed unimportant at the time. In that intensely hot summer of 1914 Americans were avidly following baseball games and tennis matches.

Europe was a long way off, and its affairs did not concern the United States.

Ever since the beginning of the century, Americans had held an illusion of peace. Voices across the country insisted that as men became better educated and more affluent, they would automatically correct social evils and permanently eliminate war. Jane Addams, establishing Hull House in one of Chicago's seamy neighborhoods, believed the juvenile delinquent to be a product of his environment. People were confident that whatever was wrong in the world they could fix by their own good sense and ingenuity. That hope shattered when war exploded in Europe in August.

William devoured the news, thanking God that President Wilson urged Americans to remain neutral in thought as well as deed. He and Minnie could go ahead with plans for their October wedding.

Chapter 3

Billy wiped the perspiration from his forehead and ran his finger around his neck to loosen his shirt collar.

"If the fellows I used to play football with could see me now, all dressed up like this, they'd never believe it."

Sam laughed. "A he-man like you nervous over a simple thing like getting married? Little Minnie is so sweet—how can you be afraid of her?"

"I'm not afraid of *her*," Billy retorted. "I'm afraid of myself. What if I can't take care of her the way I want to?"

"Well, she doesn't seem worried." Then Sam looked at his brother seriously. "I'm glad you and Minnie are getting married now instead of waiting until you get a bigger salary. That little second-floor flat you've rented isn't much with no heat or electricity, but Minnie is really fixing it up."

John came into the room, laughing. "Somebody just asked if you knew this was Friday the thirteenth and didn't you know it was an unlucky day? I said if you believed in luck, which you didn't, you'd think it was the luckiest day of your life. *I* think you're lucky to get a girl like Minnie to be willing to listen to you preach twice every Sunday for the rest of her life."

"Plus prayer meeting in the middle," Sam added, "and probably a sermon for breakfast given at the top of your lungs." Sam straightened his tie and asked, "Where are you going on your honeymoon?"

Billy looked at his innocent expression and then at John's equally bland look and retorted, "That's none of your business." Then he pleaded, "I know you'd like to get back at me for some of my practical jokes. It wouldn't matter if it was just done to me. But, please, don't spoil anything for Minnie."

The church members were delighted that their bachelor minister was marrying. They welcomed Minnie with lovely gifts to help make the small second-floor flat homey. Gas lamps softened the lack of furniture in some rooms while showing up the brand new sofa and chair in the living room. A second-hand coal stove in the kitchen and another in the dining room kept them warm on cold days.

Billy's love for fun and surprises kept Minnie anticipating each day that winter. She got used to hearing him take the stairs two at a time in the middle of the day to say, "Let's go for a ride."

That meant an El or streetcar ride into Chicago or around Morton Park or Douglas Park the way they did on their honeymoon. But the sight of men drifting aimlessly along the sidewalks or stumbling drunken in the gutters always brought Billy back to the central purpose of his life — giving out the gospel.

He handed Minnie his coat one day with a casual, "My pocket is torn again. Have you time to fix it before I leave?"

Minnie took the coat and looked up at him with a puzzled frown. "I've mended this pocket half a dozen times. I didn't know a man's pockets wore out so quickly and so often. What *do* you put in them that makes them tear?"

"Nothing. Just a few tracts."

Minnie leaned back in the chair, letting the coat lie in her lap. Her eyes twinkled up at him as she asked, "How many is a few?"

Then, seeing the wad of tracts he picked up from the table, she shook her head. "You wouldn't see enough people for all those if you walked up and down every street in Chicago's loop. Can't you carry about a fourth that number at any one time?"

"Oh, no! I need a big supply for variety. I can't just throw a tract out without a thought about a person's needs. He may need a salvation tract or one on Christian growth. Or maybe he's lonely—or discouraged—or a slave to drink—"

"All right, Bill, I see your point. Carry as many as you need, as long as you keep me supplied with thread and material to do the patching."

She smiled at him, but William looked back, his face and voice sober. "I've often wondered which one of these tracts made my father think seriously about accepting Christ. He never told me. Minnie, think of all those years Dad thought he was a Christian because he went to church and knew the Bible so well. I couldn't make him see that that wasn't enough. Then I noticed him reading a tract when he finished the newspaper and there wasn't anything else around to read. One of them finally convinced him that being good wasn't enough. That he needed to take Christ as his Saviour."

Minnie reached her hand to hold his tightly, remembering the shock of his father's death just a month after their marriage.

Billy's voice was somber as he said, "Whenever I hand someone a tract, I wonder if it will be that person's last opportunity to hear. Like Dad, starting out in the morning, anticipating a good day of business, and being killed by an El train before he got to his job."

He watched her mend his coat, thinking about tracts. He could bring that thought into a sermon. He could call the message, "A Pocket Full of Dynamite."

"Minnie, I'm going to work out a message on the importance of tracts. I'll talk about having a big enough supply to meet any need, for salvation, for Christian service, for giving. Maybe some on other religions, some in different languages. Each one should have a place a person could sign his name showing he'd made a decision, and maybe an address where he could write for counseling or more literature. The second main point would be that the person giving the tract should know its contents so he could explain it."

His moment of sorrow had passed in the excitement of planning, and he stood up. "I'll bring up several good loads of coal before I go. I want to get in some visiting this afternoon and work on several messages. I'll be home in time for supper."

Minnie raised her face for his kiss, patting his cheek. "I know better than to count on that promise."

"Oh, by the way, you'll be interested in the report the board has prepared. Mr. Klunder said anyone who thinks statistics are dull and cold should read these because they tell an exciting story." William's grin showed his agreement.

Minnie smiled as she listened to him plunge down the stairs. She remembered Mr. Klunder's enthusiastic words to her last Sunday evening after church. "We could hardly believe the figures. We were sure we'd made a mistake." She looked at the report.

Male members — 51   Female members — 111
Officers, teachers, Sunday school scholars — 240
Members in young people's society — 80
Value of church property — $6,000
Minister's yearly salary — $1,180
Amount of debt — 00

Then the report compared the figures with those of the first Sunday William had preached just fifteen months earlier. That day, twenty-five had been in the morning service; there was no young people's group or adult Sunday school; the property value was almost nonexistent; the church was in debt to the denomination and the previous minister; the five dollars to pay the visiting preacher was scraped together each week. The report went on:

> A matter of special note are the meetings held in the open air on Sunday evenings during the past summer. From 500 to 1,000 people were witnessed to each night. Out pastor has filled the pulpit in the home church regularly, conducted the Wednesday, Friday, and Saturday night meetings, attended the business meetings of the Christian Endeavor, Sunday school, and the trustees of the church. He assisted in the Sunday school and the Christian Endeavor Sunday afternoon meetings, worked in the County Hospital, and either made or had a part in making 700 calls in the field.

Minnie held the report, frowning down at it. Bill had done all this because he loved the work. But it was time to train others to do some of it. Only his unusually good health made him able to stand the pace and still think of her.

She read the final paragraph of the trustees' report to the denomination.

> Notwithstanding the fact of the church's assuming its own support and being free of any financial help during the past fifteen months, the treasurer's report shows that the test has been

endured. With the continued support of its members there is no reason why the church should not continue entirely self-supporting.

The busy winter blew itself out, and spring gradually warmed the days. Billy followed the tangled events of the war as reported in newspaper articles and editorials. Opinion ebbed and flowed as to whether America had a moral obligation to get into the fight. But the general feeling across the country was indifference.

Then in May 1915 a German submarine torpedoed the British ship *Lusitania*. No warning had been given so that lifeboats could be prepared, and almost twelve hundred passengers sank under the dark, cold waters, including 128 Americans.

Public opinion blazed, debating the rightness of Americans traveling on ships belonging to warring nations. Secretary of State William Jennings Bryan resigned in protest over the issue. The signing brought the war closer, and anti-German feelings grew.

Billy kept a wary eye on Minnie, scolding her gently as summer came and the July sun made the second-floor flat unbearably hot.

"You mustn't do so much. I don't mind if things are dusty. Don't go up and down the stairs so often. You must take care of yourself."

"Bill, I need the exercise. The doctor says it's better for me to be active. And you may not mind the dust, but I do. I *am* glad the baby will come before the August heat sets in, but really, I feel perfectly well. After all, July twenty-ninth is not too far away now." She stopped to smile at him. "However, I'm not planning to go to the church picnic on the twenty-third."

Minnie waved Billy off to the picnic that Saturday, anticipating a quiet day for herself. Suddenly she heard him pounding up the stairs; he burst into the living room, his face pale.

"Minnie!" he gasped. "A terrible accident. The Western Electric excursion—for the employees—the fancy boat—the Eastland—it turned over. Turned right over in the river. It was crowded, and hundreds of people have drowned."

"Oh, Bill! Our members who work there—only the picnic kept them from being on it."

He nodded, his face drawn. "I know. We did try to set the picnic for another day because some were so put out by the conflict. Now I'm so glad—" He stopped, his voice broken.

"Our members? Did any of them?" Minnie's voice faltered.

His face worked with emotion as he said, "I haven't heard who went on the excursion but some did. I rushed home to tell you so you wouldn't hear the news from someone else. I'm going back to see what I can do. You won't worry if I'm late?"

"No, Bill. Don't think of me now. Go where you are needed."

Minnie listened to the rush of his feet down the stairs and then stepped out onto the little porch. She watched him stride along the street until he was lost from sight.

This was what she had accepted when she said yes to his proposal of marriage. She would always have to share him with others—with the church people, with those who hurt, with those needing counsel. The words, "Don't think of me now" had sounded so brave when she had said them a few moments ago. Of course, she had meant them. But if he were in some other kind of job—

Minnie shook her head, a faint smile curving her lips. No. When she had accepted him, she had accepted his hard place of ministry also. She whispered a prayer: "Help me not to resent the calls that take him away."

Billy came home late, dropping exhausted into a chair. Minnie brought him the supper she had kept warm and listened to his grim report.

"They say now that over nine hundred people drowned. The majority were from Cicero, since so many Western Electric employees live here."

"How did it happen?"

He shook his head. "No one knows. Eye-witness accounts are confused. One man who was walking across the bridge over the Chicago River said the boat just suddenly turned over. Bodies simply slid off into the water."

"Any—any of ours?" Minnie asked the question she hadn't wanted to ask.

He nodded, naming the families somberly. "In that one, the grandmother, mother, and daughter just slipped under the boat. John couldn't reach them, though he grabbed frantically. He saved the four-year-old boy by having him put his arms around his neck and hang on while John swam to shore."

Billy sat silent for a moment and then said, "When I heard it, I couldn't help thinking that it was a picture of salvation. The only way to be saved is by trusting Jesus Christ."

His voice cracked with weariness as he added, "So many are gone from Cicero, there'll be funerals all week. The Protestant ministers are sharing the funerals for those who have no church connections. Pray that the messages I give will not only comfort but, please God, will change lives."

"Just so you save time for the baby." Minnie tried to keep her voice light, but the words wobbled, and she dissolved in tears against William's strong shoulder. It was hot, and she was tired; the tragedy had unnerved her.

Billy was still conducting funerals on Thursday the 29th when Myrtle was born, but he was home to welcome the beautiful new life.

"Our first, Minnie. I wonder what's in store for her."

His mother smiled at him as she laid the tiny blanketed bundle in Minnie's arms. "Exactly what your father asked about you."

Billy's face was sober. "But this is not an easy world to come into."

"Nor was it when you were born," she retorted. "Times were hard and worried your father."

"But now war has added to the world's problems." Billy sighed. "I can't bring myself to preach war from the pulpit the way some ministers are doing. Germany certainly must be stopped, which means we may have to get into the fight. Personally, I feel we should, because there *are* moral issues at stake. I respect William Jennings Bryan for his stand for righteousness, but I can't agree with him that we must stay out of the war. Still, regardless of my personal political views, the pulpit is the place to preach salvation, not war. The church needs are certainly keeping my busy."

In spite of his avid following of world events, Billy found them only a backdrop to the still simmering problem of the church's relationship to the denomination. When Billy urged that the church increase its missionary giving, one board member shook his head doubtfully.

"I don't know, Pastor. Remember that the denomination helped us out in the past. It wasn't much, but we'd have had to close down completely without that help. It's only fair, now that our offerings are larger, that we give something back."

"Who knows? We may need its help again someday," someone else added.

"Well, men, let's try my idea. Let's increase our giving to missions and see what happens to our work here."

"I don't see why we can't do both," the first man insisted. "Give to missions and the denomination."

Billy didn't answer. The meeting had been long as usual and everyone was getting tired and edgy. But the more he read of the denomination's drift from belief in the infallibility of God's Word, the more troubled he was about his church's connection with it. Someday the church would be forced to take a stand on the issue. "The sooner the better," he muttered as he hurried home.

In the spring of 1916 Billy handed Minnie a letter, an invitation to hold a week of meetings in St. Louis.

"How wonderful, Bill!" Minnie's face glowed with love and pride.

He shook his head in doubt, wanting to take the opportunity, yet not sure he should. "I don't like leaving you alone with another baby on the way. You'd have to carry Myrtle up and down the stairs when you go out and she's too heavy for you in your condition."

"I can stay with Dad for the week you are gone. You know my sister would love to chance to spoil Myrtle with you not there to stop her."

Minnie found the week long, missing Bill this first time away from each other. Toward the end of the week she began gathering the baby's toys scattered through the house.

Her sister called, "Minnie! Telephone. Bill's calling."

"Bill! What a surprise…When will you be home?…
Oh. Another week?…Y-yes, we're fine…We miss
you, too."

She hung back the receiver, blinking away tears before
turning to face Marie's questioning eyes.

"Bill is having such wonderful meetings, they
want him to stay another week. A Jewish lady was
saved at last night's meeting, and she is bringing her
husband tonight."

After a decent interval she escaped to the bedroom
and let the tears come. Bill didn't know how much she
had counted on his coming home. Finally she opened
her Bible to familiar, loved verses and prayed, "Help
me not to resent the times Bill is away and I am left
to care of the children. Help me to be glad when he
goes, especially when people are saved because of his
preaching of Your Word."

The meetings in St. Louis increased Billy's desire
for his church to grow and reach out. It should be
doing more than just filling the building for Sunday
services and for the midweek meetings. The offerings
for missions were coming in well, but not enough people
were out actively witnessing. He filled his messages
with exhortations, his voice loud and his fist thumping
the pulpit desk in his earnestness.

"An effective Christian church is comprised of doers
of the Word rather than mere hearers. Revival among
genuine Christians is proportioned by the measure in

which they live the truth they know. Church history records that suffering for Christ and spiritual revival travel together. God leaves us on earth after He saves us so that we might evangelize lost souls. Let's be more aggressive about reaching out for those who are lost. Don't forget that we have the message of *life*."

He talked to his officers about starting a branch church. "I remember hearing Dr. Gray say that the unchurched areas of the United States comprise one of the world's greatest mission fields. He said that when Jesus said, 'Lift up your eyes, and look on the fields, for they are white already to harvest,' He was speaking primarily of nearby fields. Well, we have nearby fields around us. People in the Drexel area, for instance. They aren't coming to our church, so we need to go to them."

"How?"

"First, by praying about it. Then we'll make a house-to-house survey of neighborhoods. We'll ask about church backgrounds and how many children might be interested in a Sunday school."

"And leave some literature, Pastor. Some tracts, perhaps a gospel portion of Scripture. And maybe a church bulletin."

"Good point," Billy agreed. "Then, if there seems to be enough interest, we'll need an organized follow-up on the contacts. Draw up a mailing list. A few key people could start a weekly Bible study and an afternoon Sunday school."

"If we start a Sunday work, we'll need a place to meet."

Billy nodded. "Let's check that out as part of the survey. If we find a family who is really hungry for the Word, they might offer the use of their living room, or their garage. Oh, one more point. When the teams visit, they must make clear what we stand for as individuals and as a church. Let folks know that we believe the Bible and that we preach Christ crucified, risen, ascended, and coming again."

"You know, Pastor, I think we'll find people ready to listen when we call. At my place of business people are worried. There's a lot of—well, I guess you'd call it 'war hysteria.' People are scared about what's going to happen even while there's a growing outcry to get into the war. I hear March eleventh has been set aside as War Sunday in churches in New York. People cheer the ministers who preach war, in Chicago as well as other places."

"I know," Billy answered. "Some talk about 'America in Armageddon' when they don't know the meaning of Armageddon. But it's true. The President is facing a declaration of war. I don't see how it can be avoided."

Later, Billy read President Wilson's message to Congress, asking for a declaration of war on Germany. He read part of it aloud to Minnie.

"The world must be made safe for democracy. Its peace must be planted upon the tested foundations of political liberty. We have no selfish ends to serve ... It is a fearful thing to lead this great peaceful people into war…But the fight is more precious than peace, and we shall fight for the things which we have always carried nearest out hearts—for democracy, for the right of those who submit to authority to have a voice in their own governments…"

He read the rest of the message silently, and then heard Minnie say, "I suppose it had to come. But—think of all the young men who must die."

Her voice choked, and Billy knew she was thinking of their baby son, Bill, whom she had just put to bed.

Chapter 4

Billy looked out at his packed auditorium the Sunday after war was declared, seeing many unfamiliar faces.

"Who *are* all these people?" someone asked.

"Some have suddenly found they need God. They're going to be called up for the army or are sending sons off, and they are worried," Billy answered. "Whatever the reason, I'm going to hit them hard with the gospel while I have the chance."

Other churches found their attendances increased, also. The 'war to end war' was suddenly layered with spiritual overtones. Ministers urged the sale of liberty bond and war savings stamps. Germany was denounced by ministers of various shades of belief, from the president of the Federal Council of Churches to the fiery, shouting Billy Sunday. They joined in blasting anyone who was troubled about the moral implications of the war. The one who expressed doubts about the rightness of the war risked verbal and physical abuse from having his house painted yellow to being beaten or tarred and feathered.

Anti-German feeling even ran to the absurd lengths of objecting to dachshunds or any dog unlucky enough to be named Fritz.

Billy saw the war as an opportunity to preach the gospel, since anxiety brought people to church. He did not preach war messages as many ministers did, but he expressed himself forcefully on the issues of the day.

"God blesses the nation that stands for righteousness," he thundered. "And along with other issues, we Christians should support the Eighteenth Amendment. We've got to fight the liquor business, and this prohibition amendment is a giant step in that fight. Those of us who live so near Chicago can see the connection between liquor and crime."

Billy was only distracted from the troubling world situation by the continuing pressure from the denomination. The periodic demand came again, asking why the church was not contributing financially since it was so evidently prospering. The church leaders drafted a frank reply.

> Since William McCarrell has come as our minister, we are no longer on the edge of survival. In fact, we have improved our property, we have established a branch work, we are the strongest Protestant work in the area, and we are giving to obey Christ's command to spread the gospel around the world.

Billy nodded agreement when the chairman read the letter for board approval. Then he said, "Men, I think we should make a stronger statement. We must make it clear that the reason we are not giving them money is because we do not agree with their doctrinal stand. It seems to me that they must prove to us that they believe the essential truths of the Christian faith if they want our money."

"Well, now, Pastor. We have to be careful here. We don't want to antagonize anyone."

"I believe in speaking the truth even if it does hurt," Billy shot back. "Think about it a minute. The denomination leaders say frankly they don't believe in the deity of Jesus Christ or His atoning sacrifice for sin. They don't accept the Bible as the infallible Word of God."

"Well, but our church is straight on that, so what does it matter about the denomination?"

"What if someone wanted to join our church but said he didn't believe that Jesus was God?"

"Well — naturally, we wouldn't accept him as a member."

"Then why should we belong to and support an organization that doesn't believe that essential fact?"

"Umm, yes. I see your point. But still we should be careful how we say it. The Bible says we should speak the truth in love."

"I go along with that as long as the truth comes out clearly," Billy answered.

So the letter went on to say:

> We, as a church, conscientiously feel that we are called of God to stand for the integrity of God's Word ... Should we, as a church, at any time be convinced that [the denomination] is behind the

propagation of these truths...we shall be delighted to share in its work. Assuring you of our willingness to help any work that we believe to be to the glory of God through Christ Jesus we remain yours respectfully.

Billy repeated the letter to Minnie as quietly as he could, remembering that she chided him for his temper which often burst out in exasperated, loud words.

"Even when you are *right*, Bill, you don't win people to your view by arguing them down or not listening to their side. Find a Scripture verse that covers the problem and begin with that. Remember how hard the times are on everyone. The war, especially inflames people so easily. Men drafted, women going to work—life isn't normal anymore."

"You're right, of course. I'd better save my energy for important matters."

He reached for the newspaper. "I wonder how much of what we read is the truth. We've been in the war now for over a year, and victory seems as far away as ever. We thought our troops would end the fighting immediately. Instead, victory seems to hang on a thread. And now we have the flu epidemic doctors are worried about. We'll have to cancel meetings if it gets much worse."

The weary months of the summer and fall dragged on until November when the country was electrified by German's surrender and went wild in armistice celebrations.

The flu which had seemed to subside after July swept back in fury in February 1919, hitting rich and poor, babies and old people. Millions were sick and thousands died, forcing churches, schools, and businesses across the country to close.

Billy was holding meetings in Texas, but he rushed home to care for Minnie and the two children, Myrtle and Billy, who were very ill.

When Minnie recovered enough to have an interest again in the world, Billy regularly brought home bits of news.

"The reports are that we've lost more people from the flu than soldiers in the war," he said, feeding her sips of broth.

"Has anyone died from our church?"

"None of our members, but some who have attended regularly. We've had many funerals in town. And Chicago, of course—" He threw out his hands, not needing to finish the sentence.

Minnie leaned back against the pillow. "I haven't even thought about the new Sunday school building since I've been sick. Is the money for it coming in?"

"Yes! We have enough money in cash and pledges to cover the entire thirty-seven thousand. That means no debt, Minnie. People have really responded in faith."

"How soon will it be ready for use?"

"By the end of the year, I'm sure." He laughed then and said, "The first Sunday you're back, you'll hear the church orchestra. They sound great."

He got up to wander restlessly around the room, not looking at her. Finally he said, "I've taken on something else, Minnie. I've been invited to teach a Bible class each Thursday evening in Racine."

"Racine, Wisconsin? Bill! That's a long way."

"But the train connections are good," he answered, his voice eager. "And I won't be away overnight. I know it will mean a rush at suppertime, Minnie. And I won't be home to help with the children's bedtime. But it will be only one night a week. Plus the evenings I'm at church meetings, of course."

"Bill, I'm afraid you take on too much. You have all those plans for the tent work this summer — the new building — the mission preaching — overseeing the Drexel church. You'll wear yourself out. I've kept track, Bill. Some days you've worked twenty hours."

"God gave me a strong body for a reason, honey. Remember — I promised God He could have all of my life. What if out of this class in Racine God should call even one person to do a great work for Him? That would be worth the sacrifice of my time and effort."

He sat down and put an arm around her thin shoulders. "And I hope worth your sacrifice, too, my dear little wife."

"Just remember that the children and I need you, too."

"God knows that," he answered, his arms circling her. "I promise that you and the children will have a large share of my time."

Billy found the promise more easily made than kept, though he was home when baby Gordon came in 1920. Life had so many opportunities for his boundless energy. Church activities and Bible classes consumed his time but not his thoughts.

Cicero did not escape the economic and racial turmoil that swept the country after the enthusiasm of the armistice had evaporated. While politicians debated the League of Nations and watched revolution change Russia, the ordinary citizen despaired over rising prices. Over 3,000 strikes in 1919 alone protested the climbing cost of living.

The economic problems resulted in racial problems when returning soldiers, unable to find jobs, blamed Negroes and aliens. Hatred flared against minorities, reviving the Ku Klux Klan with its violent anti-Jewish, anti-Catholic, white supremacy views. Cicero's large melting pot population felt the discrimination of the drive for a "one-language nation."

Chicago festered with one of the worst demonstrations of racial hatred on a blistering July day in 1919. A young Negro boy swimming off a South Side beach strayed onto the white side of the public beach. White swimmers hurled rocks at him until he drowned. In the four terror-filled days that followed, thirty-eight people died and hundreds were injured.

Though Americans gave generously to feed the starving in Europe, they no longer welcomed immigrants. The national mood turned inward. The refusal to join the League of Nations showed the nation's reluctance to be saddled with the affairs of other nations. The 100-percent-Americanism spirit blinded people's eyes to the menace of totalitarian governments in Europe.

Billy kept up with the economic and political events. In addition, his wide reading made him acutely aware of the subtle turn from Scripture in seminaries and churches. His temper exploded at statements by theologians, widely quoted in newspapers and magazines, that "The Bible is not God's Word, but is the developing religious consciousness of one people," and "The church is simply an organization for human betterment."

"What good is that going to do the drunk on Skid Row or the young person with his whole life ahead of him?" Billy fumed.

The sight of people sitting in their yards on warm summer evenings or strolling the streets precipitated the idea of putting up a tent and having meetings each evening.

"There's a good spot over on Twenty-third Place and Laramie," he said. "We'd have to clear it with city officials, of course, but that should not be hard to do. Maybe we can offset the influence of these hoodlums who seem to be closing in on us."

His enthusiasm was contagious, but one board member cautioned, "I'm all for the idea, but don't you plan to do all the preaching. We don't want you working yourself to death."

"I won't. That's the great thing about being near Moody Bible Institute. We can have a different man preach each night for the whole summer if necessary. I'll get off some letters and line up speakers."

The tent meetings emphasized the church's energy and growth and again brought a demand from the denomination for a financial contribution. This time William's letter in January 1921 was more pointed than earlier letters had been.

> The Lord is blessing us richly here. We have just spent over $3,000 in alterations, partially for the purpose of enlarging our seating capacity, and already we are more than filling it. We look forward to the erection of a much bigger building in the near future. The church is giving thousands of dollars to missions. Hundreds of dollars lie in a trust fund, waiting for an opening of another branch church. Every month there is a splendid addition to the membership, while practically every Sunday night there are decisions on the part of adults for the Lord Jesus Christ.

> There is much more that might be said, but I merely state these few facts to assure you that the church under its present policy and stand has been remarkably blessed by God. It seems to our people as if it were a divine endorsement of the conscientious stand for the truth...As I read the spirit of the congregation there is a greater determination

than ever before to sanely, yet lovingly and firmly, stand for and propagate the fundamentals of the faith once delivered unto the saints and the old-fashioned gospel of the Lord Jesus Christ. Also not to compromise one iota with the infidelity that operates under the guise of modernism, higher criticism, and advanced learning.

Billy reread the letter. This was his strongest response so far, and he knew several board members would not approve it. They would agree with the sentiments, of course, but not the way they were stated.

"Well, this letter is going out with *my* signature!" He knew his voice sounded as defiant as the thump of his fist on the stamp.

Chapter 5

It seemed to Billy that post-war Americans rushed to embrace anything that was new and different, especially in a religious sense.

The country had come out of the war undamaged economically and quickly jumped into a position as the world's leading financial center. Prosperity pushed people to a fevered pitch of materialism. Technological developments brought labor-saving devices to ease factory and home drudgery; medical research lessened disease and relieved pain. During the 1920s prosperity returned, strikes decreased, and prices gradually declined.

But ugly threads darkened the texture of American life. The theories in Charles Darwin's books, *Origin of the Species* and *The Descent of Man*, written in 1859 and 1871, became popular. They spread doubts about the biblical revelation of special creation and, therefore, about God.

Billy feared that evolution and liberalism would become tidal waves surging from seminaries into pulpits and then through the pews to sweep the unwary Christian into doubts about the basic doctrines of the Christian faith.

Albert Schweitzer's widely acclaimed book, *The Quest for the Historical Jesus*, was actually a skeptical view of the gospels. Newspapers across the country headlined Harry Emerson Fosdick's 1922 sermon "Shall the Fundamentalists Win?" as well as his book, *The Peril of Worshiping Jesus*.

Billy seized every opportunity to thunder against the errors in liberal thinking.

> They call the God of the Old Testament a bloodthirsty God who sent nations into wars which wiped out women and children. But the God of the New Testament, they say, is represented by the "gentle Jesus" who is a "great Example and Teacher" but not God. That is a totally false distinction. The God of the Old and New Testaments is one and the same.

The social gospel had troubled him ever since reading Rauschenbush's books with their application of liberal theology to the social and economic spheres of life. He studied the aims of the Federal Council of Churches and argued against them.

"Of course we should abolish child labor and set a minimum wage and have labor arbitration. But where in all that is there a call for what is really essential? They don't say anything about Christ's call to come to Him for eternal salvation. That is the important issue, and that is the business of the church."

He plunged into a leadership role in the Christian Fundamentals movement, offering his church as host for the first Chicago Fundamentals Ministers' meeting in March 1922.

Still, all the social injustices were mirrored in the neighborhoods surrounding the McCarrells. Minnie voiced her concerns to Billy one day. "We send missionaries to Africa and other countries, but I-I wonder—are we as interested in the races near us? The Negroes and—and others?"

"I think we are, Minnie. I would never refuse help to a person because of the color of his skin. I'd be the first to help a Negro group get their own church started."

He frowned then in thought and finally said slowly, "You are right, though. Many of our people give money to missions in Africa, but won't live next door to a Negro. I don't know how we can change that. But with all the prejudice, we have to remember that Cicero people are hardworking and industrious. I can't think of a single person in the church who would take charity unless he was driven to it from utter necessity."

Minnie nodded. "I remember your father saying that he had pulled himself up by his own bootstraps."

"That's true. He started out in business with nothing and built a good business by hard work. And now we are benefiting from his work." He stopped, his voice choked with emotion.

Minnie reached a comforting hand. "I know." It was the small legacy he left them that helped them get their house. She smiled at him. "It's such a help that Myrtle and Bill and Gordon have room to play."

"And I'm glad to get you out of a second floor flat with another baby on the way."

But Minnie had picked up the newspaper, sighing as she looked at the prices. "Everything is so high. Even the good wages don't keep up with the climbing prices."

Billy's face set in grim lines as he answered, "The way to get rich is to be in the liquor business. I read the other day that beer that costs five dollars a barrel to make sells for fifty dollars a barrel."

"But it's against the law, Bill! The Eighteenth Amendment makes it illegal to sell liquor—"

"But it's not illegal to buy it," he shot back. At her puzzled frown he explained, "The law says only that it is illegal to manufacture and sell liquor. When the Senate was voting on the measure, a motion was made to include words that would prohibit the purchase of liquor, but that motion was defeated. Since people want to drink, other people are going to find ways to sell it—and make money. That's why we've got all this bootlegging. It's happening all over the country, but it seems worse in Chicago. And Cicero."

Our town has the reputation of being the center of the worst gang of criminals America has ever had. And it mainly stems from the liquor traffic. That's where the money is made. Whenever there's a chance to make money, criminals gather like vultures."

He reached into his inner coat pocket and pulled out a letter. "This came to the office this morning, Minnie. Listen."

As a mother of two boys I do not know where to turn, therefore, I decided as my last recourse to come to you. I know that you are an understanding person. My problem is this. In our block is a gambling house. They have all kinds of devices for gambling. They even take bets on horses from young boys. I am ashamed, but my own two boys are involved. They are too young to work and earn their own money. They use their school lunch money for gambling in this place. It has been going full force since last May a year ago. It is operated by a widow, and there is much else that goes on.

Please, Rev. McCarrell, won't you be so kind as to have this place closed? It's a menace and a temptation to young boys and to our community. Your word means much — you have power. You come in contact with people who could close this place. Sunday last was Mother's Day, but my heart and the hearts of other mothers in this locality were far from happy.

Billy stopped reading, staring down at the letter in his clenched fist. "And this is from a member of our church."

"*You* can't have the place closed, can you?"

"Of course not!" He struck his fist on the table. "Oh, I tried. I went charging over there, and they laughed in my face. Said they ran a legitimate business. They weren't forcing people to bet. Kids who came in with money had a right to spend it any way they wanted."

"But can't the police do something?"

"I went there, too. They didn't laugh. Not to my face. But they might as well have. The police force is in cahoots with the gamblers and hoodlums."

"Bill! They promise to uphold the law."

Billy shook his head, his lips a grim line. "The stories in the Chicago newspapers about the corruption in the city government and the police force are true. Gangsters have no fear because they have the law in their pockets. Oh, not every policeman," he answered Minnie's exclamation. "But all too often judges dismiss cases against criminals because they are bribed by money or paralyzed by fear. If a gangster or the owner of some of those places gets arrested, he simply peels money off a roll of bills, slaps it down, and walks out free."

"It's not right of me to say it, but I wish they'd stay in Chicago and leave Cicero alone."

"Apparently, the new mayor in Chicago and his chief of police are trying to clean up the mess. The result is one of the worst of them, Al Capone, has moved his headquarters to Cicero. He's settled in at the Hawthorne Inn—"

"Bill! So near—just a few blocks from us. With all that, no wonder young people are confused about right and wrong."

Billy got up to pace back and forth. "We've got to

make sure our church program does everything it can to combat the evil influences around us."

"Well, the church is certainly reaching out with its truck at the Western Electric noonday meetings." She smiled. "The name 'The First Congregational Church Gospel Truck' is almost as long as the truck itself."

Billy smiled back, but his voice was sober. "And every time I look out at all the faces while I'm preaching, I wonder what's in their minds. What hurts are they living with? What heartaches? What injustices?"

He sighed. "Even some of our own people know so little about the truths of Scripture. That's why I've been preaching doctrinal messages in the morning services and presenting the gospel in the evenings. Nothing will clean up the mess in this town but the gospel of Christ. I had a letter the other day from a young minister downstate, asking what kind of messages he should preach. I told him just to preach from the Bible and he'd never run out of material."

He disappeared into the bedroom and came back with a sheaf of papers. "I'm taking all this along to study on the train to Racine this evening," he answered Minnie's questioning look. "I want to review our Sunday school materials to be sure we're doing enough in our teaching. The Sunday school committee has made recommendations—good ones, I think."

He kissed her. "Tell the children I'm missing them. Don't wait up for me."

"I won't wait up, but you know I can't sleep until you are safely home."

Studying the Sunday school materials on the train left Billy feeling frustrated. Children needed to learn so much, and the brief Sunday school hour afforded so little time. Even if a child came regularly each Sunday, it meant less than fifty-two hours of Bible teaching in a whole year. They needed so much more than that.

He sat at his desk several weeks later with a pile of correspondence before him. His secretary spoke from the open doorway.

"Pastor, are you free?"

Billy looked up and then rose as he saw the visitor. "Come in, Mary. Tell me how Tom is getting along in college. You and George must be proud of his getting a scholarship."

Her face crumpled at his words, and she looked away, blinking back tears. "Pastor, that's why I'm here. Tom is so mixed up!"

"Tell me about it."

"You know how Tom was always at church every time there was a meeting all through high school. When he chose this college, a church school—though not of our denomination, we thought it was the right choice. But now—now in the religion class the teacher said the Bible had good stories in it. But then he laughed and said that, of course, a lot of them were fairy stories. Well, Tom spoke up and said the stories were true, that every word of the Bible was true."

"And the professor ridiculed him."

She nodded. "He asked Tom about Revelation nineteen, where it describes Jesus, and he asked if Tom really believed that Jesus had a real sword coming out of His mouth. And he said, wouldn't that be a ridiculous sight? Of course, he used fancier words than that."

"And Tom didn't know what to answer?" Billy probed gently.

She dabbed at her eyes with a handkerchief. "No. And everyone else in the class laughed. Since then he's been studying biology and—Pastor, he's so mixed up! He says he must not have learned enough in Sunday school."

"Maybe the problem is that we didn't teach him enough," Billy answered.

After he had prayed with her and she left, momentarily helped, Billy sat down at the desk and pulled the pile of papers closer, shuffling through them with a weary sigh. Correspondence and reports and brochures seemed to multiply without his ever getting to the bottom of the pile. Then his eye was caught by an article written by a pastor in Pennsylvania.

"A summer Bible school program," he muttered, his enthusiasm growing as he read the details.

> The summer Bible School uses a graded Bible course. A child begins in the kindergarten and graduates into the first grade course. As a pupil progresses normally in public school education, he will at the

same time complete a definite course in the Summer Bible School and receive and eight-year diploma. This same pupil can then take a course prepared for those of high school age.

During these years proper records of work accomplished are filed. Parents are notified through weekly report cards of their child's work. The course covers such vital teaching a Bible history, Bible geography, missions, the fundamental doctrines of the Christian faith, and the second coming of Christ. A special five-year course can be taken by those who are beyond high school age. And a special two-year, post-graduate and Teacher Training course is offered those who compete the full school curriculum.

His eyes skimmed over the rest of the information, picking up phrases. Teachers follow public school methods... courses in printed form... adequate supplies....

His secretary came to the office door to see what his exclamations were about, and saw him dialing the Sunday school superintendent's number.

"I know he's not home, but I want his wife to have him call me the minute he walks in this evening."

He hurried home through the January cold, eager to share the summer Bible school idea with Minnie and anticipating the lunch she would have ready. He thought ruefully of the chiding remark the doctor had made at his last checkup, "You are getting too heavy," and his answer, "How can I diet on Minnie's good cooking?"

He stayed to wipe dishes for her and to talk over another plan.

"Something else has been simmering in my mind. I want to strengthen the Saturday evening men's prayer meetings and make it a study and report time. I have an idea I want to try as soon as I'm off this committee that's bringing William Jennings Bryan to Moody Church later this month."

Minnie's sigh was half pride, half dismay. "Bill, you *do* manage to get involved in everything that goes on!"

"It puts an extra burden on you, Minnie, I know. Once again I'm leaving things at home to you. If any man knows the truth of the verse in Proverbs thirty-one that 'the heart of her husband doth safely trust in her' it's I."

Minnie looked up at him, her eyes misting. "That's my share in your work, Bill."

"I don't want to be gone from you and the children so much. But with world conditions as they are, we've got to promote the cause of Christ in every way possible. That's why I agreed to be on this committee to get Bryan to Chicago. He's a world figure. He's been Secretary of State, he's run for President, yet he stands for Christ fearlessly. He told a group of students that they should remember that the fear of God is the beginning of wisdom."

Before Billy left early for Chicago, the morning of the meeting, Minnie asked, "Will I be able to get a seat at the meeting tonight? I can't come early because I want to be home until the children come from school."

"Come as soon as you can. I have to be with Mr. Bryan at a noon luncheon at the YMCA, and then at an afternoon meeting at Moody Bible Institute. The committee is to have dinner with him before the evening service. Dr. Gray is so punctual, he'll see that we are at the church in plenty of time. I'll save you a seat."

A policeman barred her way with a gruff, "Sorry, ma'am. Place if full. Doors are locked."

Minnie's voice was almost lost in the noise as she said, "My husband is saving me a place. He's on the committee—"

The policeman pulled a card from his pocket, holding it at arm's length. "Mc—McCarrell. That right? OK. Duck around that door back there. Your husband said to watch out for you."

Clutching her purse under one arm and holding on to her hat, Minnie squeezed past shoving people. William stood, holding the door open a crack, and smiled with relief. "Just in time, Minnie. Look at this crowd. More than we dared hope for."

Minnie was caught in the excitement of the meeting as the packed auditorium responded to Bryan's oratory. But mostly she watched Bill on the platform with the other great men.

She looked at him the next day, concern in her eyes. "You'll feel let down now that the big event is over."

"No, I don't think so. Oh, the rally was great and, I hope, will have lasting results. We certainly got good newspaper publicity. The *Chicago Tribune* calls it 'The greatest religious demonstration that has occurred in Chicago for over twenty years.'"

Minnie laughed. "Myrtle was excited to see your picture in the paper with Mr. Bryan. She doesn't know who *he* is, but she's sure he must be important if he had his picture taken with you."

Billy got up to move around the room restlessly. "I don't feel let down. So many exciting and important things are going on. And, after all, the church is my main job."

Minnie's mouth curved in a smile. "I can see it is," she teased. "Along with your Bible classes and tract ministry and tent program and mission preaching—"

"But the church comes first, Minnie," he insisted. "It's always first. Remember I said I had an idea for a new Saturday program? Well, I've been thinking about the Lord's command that we're to be fishers of men. I believe lots of Christians would be fishers of men—that is, soul winners—if they knew how. So I thought of turning the Saturday's prayer meeting into a working meeting, a training meeting—a report meeting on what has been done for Christ during the week. The men are enthusiastic about it. In fact, we had so much discussion that the meetings didn't break up until almost two in the morning."

"William! Those meetings always last too long. You forget that most of the men get up early for work the next morning."

"But look at this, Minnie. What do you think of the idea?"

She glanced down the pages of rough notes, reading snatches aloud. "Meet Saturday afternoon at four P.M… singing and prayer… reports of witnessing… fellowship supper at six or six-thirty."

She looked at him. "Who will cook the supper?"

"We haven't thought through all the details. I don't know—maybe ask the women to take turns? No—wait—why not let the men do it themselves? We've got some good cooks—" He stopped and demanded, "What's so funny?"

"I'm just thinking about anyone who might want a Saturday wedding. If the men cook, the whole church will smell of sauerkraut and sausage."

He laughed with her, but said, "We may have to cut down on Saturday weddings. If this meeting grows, as I hope it will, there won't be room for Saturday wedding receptions."

"But what about the ladies' prayer meeting here at the house Saturday evenings? Should I discontinue that?" She sighed. "It is a rush to get the children's Saturday night baths over and get them settled in bed before the women come. One or another of the children always wants another drink or water or one more story."

"I've been thinking of that, dear. I've decided to run home for a few minutes after the fellowship supper and before the prayer meeting starts, and help you with the children. I know I don't spend time with them as I should. If they all turn out right, I'll be the first to know that it's because of your efforts."

"The children know you love them, Bill. But you are gone so much. I don't want them thinking of you only as the one who does the spanking."

He chuckled. "They need it from time to time, don't they? They wouldn't if they had inherited more of your nature than of mine. I think we'll have to call you the mayor of McCarrellville, and I'll be the chief of police."

After a moment, his voice reflective, he said, "But I am learning to channel my temper and use it against evil. And I hope the Fishermen's Club will be an effective tool against evil. This town needs it."

Chapter 6

The Fishermen's Club should have been launched on July 4 instead of October 1923, because it zoomed off like fireworks. It quickly became the zealous working organization Billy had hoped it would be. Its goals, stated in the constitution, "to win the lost and encourage and instruct the saved in service," were reached in a variety of ways. Regular members turned in weekly report sheets listing the Sunday school or Bible classes they taught, the number of persons they witnessed to, the personal calls they made, the number of tracts they distributed.

The qualifications for membership were narrow, yet wide enough to take in any man who wanted to be a fisherman for Christ: soundness in the faith, the absence of any hobby that would hinder a person's effective work for the salvation of souls, good common sense, a Christ-honoring personal testimony, a consistent Christian life, a passion for souls, and the attitude of love expressed in 1 Corinthians 13.

Some of the members were inexperienced in witnessing, and others were naturally timid; those Billy tried to help. He took an enthusiastic part in the report hour, and reminded the men, "To fish for men, you must fish. Every contact is an opportunity. If you want to keep fresh, fragrant, and fruitful, you must never quit working for souls. Whether you can talk or not, give out God's Word—*it* talks! The best way to convince a fellow that you have a Sword is to stick him with it."

One day he pulled a newspaper clipping from his pocket. "Listen, men, here's the place to give out tracts. They've counted the number of people going along the sidewalks in the loop and they estimate—so it says here: 'Two thousand pedestrians per foot of sidewalk width per hour.' It goes on to say 'No other sidewalks in the world are as busy as those in the heart of the loop.' Let's get teams in on those streets."

"We sure need a bunch of teams right here in Cicero," a member spoke up.

Billy nodded. "We've all read the Chicago newspaper accounts of the racket Al Capone has in our town. He's what—thirty-seven? And he has total power over the police and the politicians. He controls a hundred or more gambling dens, countless brothels, saloons, and speakeasies. The city government is really run by Al Capone out of the Hawthorne Inn instead of the mayor and other elected officials from City Hall."

You can see that in what he did just last week. Stormed into City Hall, threw the mayor down the stairs, and kicked him as he lay there on the sidewalk. And nobody lifted a finger to help the mayor. The police just stood around, looking the other way."

"The newspapers are in his pocket, too," Billy added. "If they object, he shuts them down simply by wrecking their equipment. They estimate he's made twenty million dollars off people like those who live around us."

Another man's voice was bitter as he added, "He claims his liquor business is legitimate. He says he makes his money by supplying a public demand for a product. Says he customers are some of the 'best' people in Chicago and if he is guilty of breaking the law, so are they."

Billy listened to the indignant comments and then said, "Yet, *we* know God is more powerful than Capone, or any tool of Satan. And I've got proof right here today. You all remember reading about the mail robbery that took place a couple of years ago at the Santa Fe station in Chicago? Well, let me introduce the man who did it."

Chairs creaked and feet shuffled as the men craned to see the slight figure that walked to the front of the room.

The man cleared his throat nervously as he said, "Several years ago I had a responsible job handling the mail at the station. On the outside I looked like your average decent citizen. But I had another side. I was part of the horrible muck of the underworld. My gang decided to go for big money and steal government mail. Since I was a 'trusted' employee, I was able to let the gang know when a big packet of government bonds and cash was coming through. I won't go into all the details, but the heist was successful. We were in the clear until one of the gang cashed one of the stolen war bonds and gave the whole thing away."

He looked around at the intent listeners. "I know you're wondering how come I'm here at Fishermen's Club. Well, God put an ex-con turned evangelist on my case while I was in jail waiting to be sentenced. This ex-con had been saved here in Fishermen's Club, and he came to the jail and hammered John three sixteen at me. I accepted Christ as my Saviour. I was free inside even though I knew I'd be spending a lot of my life a prisoner in jail."

Billy interrupted. "Saving you was one miracle, but God did another, too. Tell us how you got out of jail."

"I'd been in jail about thirteen months but hadn't been officially sentenced. The US marshall they sent to bring me into Chicago for sentencing got drunk on the way and was fired. Then when I finally appeared another day in court, the judge got sick. The judge who was supposed to take his place, didn't show up. Finally, the attorney told me that I was a free man since I hadn't been sentenced. He gave me some money and told me to go. Believe me, I didn't argue."

"What are your plans now?" Billy asked.

"To go into jails and tell men what God did for me. And I'm here in Fishermen's Club to learn how to witness. I—I have to say one more thing. You've probably only seen the Hawthorne Inn from the outside.

You've looked at the windows that are shuttered by steel bars. *I've* been in it. I've been through those electrically-operated doors. They swing in instead of out to give extra protection to the gangsters. And—and *fearful* things go on inside. But here, this church has its doors standing wide open, inviting people to come in. God is using this place. And He's using *you*, the Fishermen's Club. I belong to God because of this organization."

In the silence that followed, someone began singing,

> Rescue the perishing, care for the dying,
> Snatch them in pity from sin and the grave;
> Weep o'er the erring one, lift up the fallen,
> Tell them of Jesus the mighty to save.

"There we have it, men," Billy said quietly. "We talk about the liquor and gambling and vice that surrounds us. But it all goes back to the basic problem of sin. Let's fight it, men. Fight it with the sword of the Sprit which is the Word of God. But remember—we're not fighting *men*; we're fighting *sin*. We hate the sin, but we love the sinner."

No one living in Cicero had to look far to see the evil epitomized by Al Capone and his hoodlums. When gun battles erupted suddenly in Cicero streets between rival gangs, citizens cowered wherever they could find shelter from the rain of bullets.

During the city's 1924 election Capone's gunmen patrolled the polling places in order to keep in office a mayor he could control. When the polls opened, cars with armed gangsters cruised the streets. Voters were beaten, some shotgunned to death, and paper ballots torn to shreds if they were marked with the wrong name. Policemen from Chicago rushed to Cicero to stop the violence. Just at dusk police and gangster met at a polling place with blazing guns. Al Capone's brother, Frank, was killed and later eulogized at a funeral lavish with $20,000 worth of flowers.

Onlookers wondered if anyone could stop Capone and the others. Billy preached that only Jesus Christ could. "No matter who you are, or how low you have sunk in sin, Jesus Christ will free you. Simply come to Him."

Billy had scarcely begun that invitation on a cold winter Sunday evening when a man walked unsteadily down the aisle, pulling a gun from one pocket and a bottle of liquor from another. Men in the congregation jumped to intercept the ragged figure, his shoes tied with rope.

But the man held the gun and the bottle out to Billy. "I've belonged to Capone," he said, his voice slurred and broken. "But now I want to belong to Jesus Christ."

Billy put his arm around the man's shoulders and led the people in thanking God for His new child.

Billy walked home from the church office one afternoon the next week, hands jammed in his pockets against the cold, his mind burdened with a critical letter he had just received. A thud in the middle of his back stopped him short, and he turned around just as another well-aimed snowball lifted his hat. As the next-door children ducked behind their snow fort, he scooped up snow and pelted them back, rushing their fort to grab some of the ammunition they had made in advance. Other neighbor children rushed out to join the fun, some siding with him to even the odds. Finally he brushed off his hat and went home, the letter no longer important.

But he couldn't forget problems for long. Everywhere he looked he saw moral decay. But increasingly the theological and spiritual issues vexed him even more than the political and social issues. He found himself warning his people against the materialism of the age, but most of all thundering against apostasy, a word he used frequently.

"We must hold to the fundamentals of the faith. The Holy Spirit urges Christians to fight against apostasy by building themselves up in the most holy faith. The best defense against apostasy is aggressive, constructive attack. History records that the tide of the war changed from defeat to victory within three days. German leaders, who on the first of those three days were planning division of the fruits of victory, on the third day conceded defeat among themselves. During those three days, two American divisions with a division of Algerian soldiers hurled back the German lines and maintained their advance positions. A similar Christ-honoring attack upon biblical apostasy in every form is due our Lord and Savior, Jesus Christ."

A harsh letter a few days later accused him of using the pulpit to preach politics.

"I never bring politics or current events into the pulpit except as illustrations," he answered indignantly. "My job is to preach the gospel."

"But you could be more tactful," Minnie urged softly. "You won't get people to agree with you by hitting them over the head with arguments."

"I know." He sighed. "I guess I haven't gotten rid of my temper after all. But when I see all that's going on in the world and in some churches, it makes me boil. I get so—"

"Bill!"

He swallowed his burst of words and grinned back at her.

His blood boiled again in the hot summer of 1925 as he read newspaper accounts of the Scopes trial in Dayton, Tennessee. He read snatches of newspaper columns aloud to Minnie, his voice quivering with anger, and then crumpled the newspaper.

"Here's this man Scopes, a biology teacher, arguing for evolution in violation of the state law, to say nothing of the violation of God's law. And he's got this Clarence Darrow as his attorney. Darrow claims that 'intellectual freedom is on trial. Learning and common sense are at stake.'"

He looked at Minnie, the newspaper clenched in his fist. "People think they are being intellectual and scientific if they believe in evolution. Darrow's trying to make a mockery of creation. He's trying to show Bryan as an ignoramus because he stands for the Genesis account of creation. Well, one thing's sure. The sympathies of the people in the courtroom are with Bryan. He's sure to win the case."

Billy's prediction came true as Scopes was found guilty and fined. But Billy snorted his opposition to Darrow's claim that the Scopes trial had forever discredited fundamentalism. "Not as long as those of us who believe God's Word are willing to stand up and be counted. They called the jury 'twelve uneducated hillbillies trying to decide scientific matters.' Well, those of us who believe the Bible have to prove we're not ignoramuses. We can do it if we stand together. All fundamentalists must stand together against the forces of liberalism and apostasy."

He came home a week later, his voice heavy with emotion. "Bryan is dead. The paper says it was the heat in Tennessee and the pressures of the case that caused it." He stopped, looking down at the article before he went on, "It also says the ridicule Darrow heaped on Bryan was too much 'for the proud man whose great career centered in moral idealism.' Bryan didn't believe in mush like that. He was centered in Christ, and that's what made him great."

He turned to Minnie. "I tell you, the world would squeeze us into its mold if it could. The extreme fashions we see, the movie craze, and the wild music. This writer Fitzgerald—his novels are grabbed by young people. I'm glad the Sunday school has taken a stand on worldly amusements. They're asking the teachers and officers not to attend movies as an example."

"Did that come out of the discussion about not showing films in church?"

He nodded. "Some argued that missionary films should be shown in the church. But I don't believe we should make any exceptions. If someone wants to show missionary pictures they can do it in a private home. Let's keep everything of that kind out of the church."

"Not everyone will agree," Minnie warned.

"I know. It bothers me that membership in the average church is more easily procured than membership in the average worldly organization. Sometimes you can't tell the difference between a Christian and a non-Christian. This jazz age that papers talk about does affect all of us, whether we want it to or not. The movies and the drinking and the smoking, even by women—"

He stopped, shaking his head. "Sometimes I wonder how I can attack both matters—separation from the world and separation from those who deny Christ."

"I like that outline for the message you're giving at the young people's conference next weekend. Our own children, from newborn Paul to Myrtle, have to be trained to avoid even the appearance of evil."

Billy frowned in thought. "That may be the hardest of all with the Bible ridiculed as it is today. I can't understand the indifference of Christians to what is taking place in the denominations — all of them. The seminaries turn out men who scarcely believe anything. And if the ministers don't believe God's Word, it won't be long until the people don't. I'm coming more and more to believe that we must take a stand against denominational apostasy."

"You can't do it by yourself," Minnie protested.

"There are others who agree with me. I'm getting letters constantly from ministers around the state who are fed up with the drivel they read and hear from their denominational leadership. I've talked to a number of men in Grand Rapids the last few times I've gone for my Bible class. They are concerned, too."

"Well, your main responsibility now is to the new building. When that is finished, you'll have time to think of other matters."

He smiled at her. "You're right, as usual. What would I do without you? You take care of the house and the children, feed me too well—"

"Bill, I enjoy our children. Of course, I wish you were home more to enjoy the good times we have. Yesterday we all took the street car out to LaGrange and had ice cream cones. It was fun. Everything we touched on the streetcar coming home got sticky because I forgot to take a wet washcloth along."

The back door slammed, and Bill called from the kitchen, "Mother?"

"In here."

They heard the lid of the cookie jar rattle before Bill came in, his mouth full, one arm circling a football.

"Hi, Dad, didn't think you'd be home. Hey—will you show me how to throw a pass? Mother's getting pretty good at baseball 'cause we play a lot after supper. But she's not so good at football."

"Not right now, son. I've got to go—"

"William!"

He looked at Minnie, heard the warning in her voice, and stood up, grabbing the football. "First, you pull your arm back like this and then you—"

"William! Bill! Out of the house with that ball."

Minnie shut the door behind them and stood listening, knowing the yard would soon be swarming with neighbor children running to get in on the impromptu game.

Billy bounded in from the office at noon the next day, handing Minnie a letter, but not waiting for her to read it. "They want me to be a member of the Board of Trustees of Wheaton College. Imagine! Me!"

Minnie scanned the letter and looked at him. "Dr. Blanchard wants you on the board because he says, 'Billy McCarrell is a man of prayer.' Oh, Bill, I am proud of you."

"Don't be, Minnie. It's all the grace of our wonderful Lord." He grinned then as he added, "I'm sure there are plenty of people I rub the wrong way who will keep me humble."

The church grew so rapidly that everyone could see a new building was needed. The prosperous times made $33,500 for six vacant lots on which to build seem too good a deal to pass up.

"Everyone knows we need the building, so money is coming in well in gifts and pledges. It should be paid for by the time it is finished."

"The ground-breaking ceremony was so impressive," Minnie said. "And I thought Dr. Buswell's message was just right. He's a good successor to Dr. Blanchard as president of the college. I'm glad little Ruth's arrival didn't make me miss it."

Billy prowled around the new building as it grew, eager for its completion.

"We're building just at the right time," one of the board members exulted. "The economy is so strong, and people have so much money that it's easy for them to give."

"You don't read the same reports I do, apparently," another man argued. "Sure, American production and profits are high. But it's an uneven prosperity. I hear talk about growing unemployment. All these high tariffs to protect American goods from foreign competition—" He shook his head again. "The economy hasn't been right since the war ended."

"And what about the unlimited speculation we're seeing in the stock market?" another man asked, worry sharpening his voice. "People are investing every penny wild over the idea of buying stocks on margin. There are increasing rumblings about the market being unstable—"

"Poppycock!" The man's voice boomed with confidence. "My broker tells me we're rising a crest of prosperity in this country greater than the world has ever seen. All the financial wizards keep saying that we'll all be rich. The papers quoted Bernard Baruch to that effect just yesterday. If anyone knows, he does."

Billy's voice rose over the heated exchange. "Men, let's not get too dependent on money. Let's remember that all we have is from the Lord's hand. He *is* blessing us. But I believe it is because during these years we have sent ten of our young people to the foreign field and are supporting them fully. That is more evidence of our growth than the new building. God is working in and through our church because we are faithful to Him and His Word. If we drift from Him, the blessing will stop."

The men nodded agreement and listened to the chairman's report of the plans for the dedication of the building.

"It's set for the last Sunday in September. We want the whole community to know what's going on. We're planning the move to be a parade with a police escort as we march from the old building to the new. I estimate that enough people will be marching that the first ones in the parade will be seated in the new auditorium while others are still coming from the old building. The flags everyone will carry will make it look very colorful."

Billy stood to his feet. "I want to express my heartfelt gratitude to God for you men, for your loyal and sacrificial service. Without you and the officers and leaders of the various organizations and the loving and united church membership, this work would not exist. It is not *my* work; it's *our* work under God."

The Sunder school superintendent led the men on a tour of the new classrooms. "They're ready just in time to get the fall program off with a bang. Here we are—1929. When I think back fifteen years to that tiny, dark Sunday school room in the original building, I see what God has done for us."

Rejoicing over the new building went on. But in early October several men in the church came to Billy with their concerns. They had small businesses and were struggling to survive.

"Pastor, I don't see how people can go on talking about prosperity. Lots of businesses are going under. And at the same time the stock market soars higher every day. *Are* things going to be all right, Pastor?"

"Not from what I read," Billy answered. "International affairs are in a hopeless mess. European nations can't—or won't—pay their war debts and reparations. I think we're going to see the truth of the Scripture which warns against trusting in uncertain riches."

The crash of the stock market came three weeks later

on October 24, Black Thursday. Billy and his board met in grim session.

The treasurer rose to give his report, his face and voice gloomy. "We have to keep up the payments on the building. We can't allow the bank to foreclose. But that's not our only problem. Not only are we saddled with payments for the new building, but we've got the old one dragging on us as well. Who's buying anything now? Especially on old, rundown church building."

"We'll just have to let it stand empty—"

"That's not the problem," the treasurer snapped, frustration edging his voice. "The thing is we've got to keep it in fairly good shape against the day that someone might want to buy it. And that's going to cost money. The gutters and windowsills are rotting. Other repairs are needed. Especially painting before the hard winter sets in."

"How about praying that the next millionaire who jumps out a window will leave us whatever money he has?" The attempt at humor met with withering glances.

"It's just one more matter to bring to the Lord," Billy finally reminded them. "He's got the answer. We simply have to wait for it."

Whenever he walked past the old building, Billy prayed, "Lord, help us."

The answer came as fire sirens shrieked one night, and Billy was yanked from sleep by the shrill telephone ring.

"Pastor! The old church was struck by lightning. It's on fire!"

Chapter 7

Billy threw on clothes and raced to the building, standing in stunned shock. How could *this* be God's answer to their earnest prayer?

"We aren't using the building, of course, but we can't afford to lose it by fire and not get anything out of it," he said to the others standing by in gloom.

But at the board meeting the next evening, the treasurer bounded up, excitement plain on his face. "I dug out the insurance policy on the building to see what we could salvage." His face broke into a smile. "You're not going to believe this, but one of the clauses covers loss by fire, *fire caused by lightning!*"

"Thank God!" Billy exclaimed fervently. "That will give money enough tor necessary repairs and allow us to keep the building in shape until a buyer comes along. Wait—let me change that. Until God sends a buyer along."

"In the meantime, we've got problems." The treasurer cleared his throat and adjusted his glasses. "The fact is that we have a building fund debt of one hundred sixty-five thousand at six percent interest. And we have a nine thousand dollar payment due in two months."

"Does that come due before or after Christmas?"

"Just before. As to other expenses, most of you know that we need about fourteen hundred each month for salaries, lighting, heating, postage, and secretarial help. And we spend about the same amount each month for missions. That last figure includes some mission outreach into the community, which we could consider cutting back."

Billy stood up, shaking his head. "Let's not even talk retreat at this point. Let's think of what we *can* do, not what we can't."

"But Pastor Billy, we must be practical. We can't expect people to give if they have to go without food to do it. So many of our people pledged money in good faith, but simply can't pay. They want to meet their pledge, but they don't have the money."

"I've been hit hard," another man said. "I've worked at Western Electric for eighteen years. Now I'm out. They've cut their employees from thirty thousand to six thousand. We've got a little saved, but when that's gone, well—" His voice trailed off as he sat down.

"Still—we have to remember that we're giving to God, not to the church," a man began diffidently, and Billy exclaimed, "That's it exactly! I believe 1 Peter 1:7 applies here. Jim, read it, will you?"

"That the trial of your faith, being much more precious than of gold that perisheth, though it be tried with fire, might be found unto praise and honour and glory at the appearing of Jesus Christ."

Billy nodded. "We are experiencing the trial of our faith in a very practical way. The question is, Do we trust God to supply our needs?"

"The people are discouraged, though, Pastor. This is a working-man's town. A lot of men have been laid off, and others know it's just a matter of time until they are, too. They don't have reserves—"

"Reserves!" snorted another. "Everybody's reserves crashed."

"What little money people have goes for shoes and coal and rent."

Billy nodded. "I know. I've listened to so many of our people, prayed with them." His voice dragged with fatigue. Then he burst out, "But *God* knows, too. We've got to put our confidence in Him, the sovereign God."

The financial plight of the people and the debt on the church building burdened Billy. But a heavier burden was the continuing danger he saw in theological liberalism. Other ministers in the Chicago area agreed with him and met frequently for mutual encouragement.

"The liberal idea takes the Bible out of its place of authority in a person's life and puts experience there instead. That's what worries me the most." The young minister shook his head, discouragement shadowing his voice.

"I agree," Billy interjected. "I do a lot of reading to keep abreast of theological thinking, as I'm sure you all do also. I find that liberals invade schools on the pretense of academic freedom, and then work against any view but their own. They call us militant and divisive because we won't swing with them and deny Scripture. And this denial of the Bible as God's Word is the basic heresy, of course. They scoff at the idea of original sin and at anything miraculous or supernatural, including Christ's atonement. And, of course, the idea of His bodily second coming is foreign to them."

"You know, Billy, thinking of your reference to the supernatural. Don't you wonder at people? I hate to admit it, but two of my families, long-time members, people I thought I could count on to recognize error, have been taken in by this Theosophical Society. They're swept up in the 'psychic and spiritual powers latent in man.' That's a quote from one of my last conversations with them."

Another minister nodded. "Some of these groups have been around quite awhile, but are suddenly growing. I suppose it's because of the hard times—the uncertainties—fear of the future. People are turning to Unity, to Christian Science—"

"But why don't they turn to the Bible?" Billy pounded the desk in his frustration. "Those of us who preach it had better begin to stand by it, defend it. Show people it has the only answer to any problem."

The minister next to him leaned forward as he said, "I've got a man in my church, a teacher, a serious, earnest man, who's sold on Karl Barth." He stopped to give a wry grin. "I have got confess I'm not up on Barth, but at least he's an antidote to the social gospel stuff we've heard for so long. Barth believes in God, certainly."

Billy spoke swiftly, not stopping to choose his words. "Barth is as bad in his way as any of these others. In some ways he's worse, because the unwary can mistake what he really teaches."

"Well, now, that's a bit extreme, Billy."

"I mean it. I come back always to the heart of the matter. What does a man or a church or a denomination teach about the deity of Christ and the authority of the Bible? That's the crux. Everything else stands or falls on those two points. Barth does emphasize the Bible. But he sees it as a book that becomes the Word of God to a person *if* that person finds it so. If the Bible meets a need at a certain time, then it is the Word of God to him. Barth does not believe that the Bible is God's Word in an objective, historical sense."

One man had the last word as the meeting broke up. "It seems as though all the denominations are going under theologically. Thank God some men are taking a stand like those who have pulled out of Princeton Seminary. The time may come when more of us will have to pull out."

Billy echoed the words. With the economy worsening, the church still faced demands from the denomination for money. Billy faced the issue with his board, trying to reassure them.

"You know we don't owe the denomination a cent. We've long since repaid the thousand dollars it gave for the property years ago. We're entirely self-sufficient. Our only obligation is to remain true to God and His Word."

He looked around the circle of men, his voice serious as he said, "I want you to know that I've given a great deal of thought and prayer to our situation as a church. I've searched the Bible for guidance. As I understand it, Scripture abounds with warning concerning the fearful apostasy that will characterize the last days, apostasy that will prepare the world for Antichrist. God's Word exhorts saved ones to separate from apostasy even more forcibly than it exhorts them to separate from carnality. Apostasy creates carnality. Its ultimate aim and endeavor is to eliminate the Bible, which, if successful, would eliminate God."

He took a deep breath and, holding his voice steady, said, "I'm going to propose that we completely sever relations with the denomination."

"Can we do that legally?" came a doubtful question.

Another cautioned, "Now wait a minute. As long as we don't bother them and they don't bother us — too much anyway — why stir up a hornet's nest? We've already changed our name to the First Independent Congregational Church of Cicero. That shows don't go along with the denomination in everything. We're independent, sure, but we have to belong *somewhere*."

Billy felt himself flushing and knew his temper was rising, but he controlled his voice as he agreed. "No, we don't want to cause unnecessary trouble. But if you'd read the things I have lately, heard the statements by Congregational ministers denying that Jesus is God, that He died to save us, that miracles happened—" He stopped, too choked with anger to finish.

"But, Pastor, *we* know those statements are false. Our people know the truth. You've taught us so well. We're not going to be swayed by any of that."

"I see what the pastor is getting at," another man spoke up. "When people hear our church name, they just automatically assume that we go along with those ideas. That right, Pastor?"

"Exactly. Oh, I know it's not just our denomination that teaches these heresies. And they've been around for a long time. These ideas are not modern at all in the sense of being new. They are as old as Lucifer. Way back in the Garden of Eden, Satan cast doubt on God's Word. What we are seeing today is a mushrooming of apostasy, this sharp turn from God and His Word."

He stopped, looking at the sober faces of the men he worked with and loved. His face broke into a smile. "Thank God for His promise in Isaiah fifty-nine nineteen that 'when the enemy shall come in like a flood, the Spirit of the LORD shall lift up a standard against him.' I believe God will do just that for those who are courageous enough to take a stand against apostasy."

"You're certainly involved in the fight, Pastor. You've been part of the World Fundamentals Movement and have gone out speaking around the country. I like their slogan, 'Sound the Alarm.'"

Billy chose his words carefully as he answered, "I appreciate everything that organization is doing in its fight for the truth. But lately—" He hesitated and then said slowly, "Lately, I've wondered if it is enough just to alert believers within various denominations to the dangers they face. I believe we should begin to urge believers to cut denominational ties.

He took several sheets of paper from an inside coat pocket. "Here is the action taken by our denomination that forced me to believe that we must pull out. The Congregational denomination has passed a resolution favoring a union between it and the Universalists."

"Universalists? What do they believe?"

"Let me put the core of their teaching as simply as possible. They believe God is going to save everyone. Since Christ died for all men, all will be saved, even if they have not personally accepted Him as Savior."

"That's not what the Bible says!" came the indignant response.

"It is not. According to their view, we are wasting money sending out missionaries and the missionaries are wasting their time and effort. This is why I propose that we cut loose. This resolution shows how far the denomination has gone into apostasy."

"Well, that does put a different light on your proposal, Pastor. Let's give it some prayer."

"I've contacted a few other sound men in the denomination. We're sending a booklet to every Congregational minister in the state to warn explicitly of the biblical errors of Universalism."

"You won't be thanked for your efforts," one man predicted.

He was right. The attack on Billy and the other sound men came in bitter letters and phone calls. The criticism added weight to the weary winter of 1929 that dragged itself out. Snow piled up in yards and made sidewalks and streets hazardous. The devastation of the stock market crash oppressed everyone with gloom. In it all Billy was grateful for Minnie's skillful managing of the home and six children without burdening him with demands.

But she worried about him and gently scolded, "Bill, you go constantly. It's not just the physical work. I know you are strong and healthy. It's the way you throw yourself into everything you do—the preaching and mission work—and your weekly classes in Racine and Grand Rapids and other places. You wear me out just watching you."

"Come now, Minnie. Everyone knows that a mother of six young children works harder than anyone. *You* don't sit down from morning until night. Anyway, I'm enjoying the work. I can't think of anything I'd give up."

"How can you enjoy the trouble — the commotion — the controversy?"

"I don't enjoy controversy, Minnie. Well — yes, I guess I do in a way. But not for controversy's sake," he added hastily. "I simply can't stand at the edge of the battle and not take part, especially when the battle is so crucial. Sometimes I feel almost like Joshua demanding, 'Who is on the Lord's side?' I believe we must be willing to stand up and be counted, no matter what the cost."

She sighed. "I'm glad the board and the members are with you in this fight over denominational control."

"I am, too. We've talked about it and prayed over it. I believe the situation has come to a head. We're having an official board meeting on Monday, February third. I'm making it clear that the purpose is to consider reasons in favor of our severing completely from the denomination."

"Will that mean we will have to just stand alone as a church?"

"I know of a small group in the St. Louis area called the American Conference of Undenominational Churches. Possibly, we could unite with them. I had a letter several months ago, last September in fact, asking if we and other independent churches would join their conference."

"Many of our people would feel better belonging somewhere. I know I would."

"We're going to meet for prayer at seven-thirty — earnest prayer, Minnie — for God's guidance.

We don't want to do anything rash. I expect it will be a long meeting."

She laughed at him across the table. "Is *that* unusual?"

But his concern for the step and its consequences showed in his serious face as he ignored the teasing and pleaded, "Minnie, keep on praying with me about this. I've wrestled with this issue for so long. I don't want to lead the church to a wrong decision. I know we fundamentalists are accused of being divisive because of our stand on Scripture. But how can we do otherwise? God's Word is God's Word. They make us out to be anti-intellectual because we defend the Bible. But an anti-intellectual refuses criticism out of fear that he will be proven wrong. That's not our position. I welcome a chance, *any* chance to explain my stand on the Bible."

The unanimous result of the board meeting was a resolution to be presented to the membership.

> Whereas the Congregational Conference of Illinois at its last Annual Meeting (May 1928), definitely committed itself to organic union with the Universalist Church…[and] sought, to the full extent of their authority, to commit our churches to a general approval of the doctrines held by, and to organic union with the Universalist churches (a church holding a system of doctrine commonly regarded by the evangelical Christian denominations to be so at variance with the Word of God and the historic faith of the New Testament Church, as to prevent its recognition as orthodox, and,

therefore, outside their Christian fellowship). BE IT RESOLVED, that we, the First Congregational Church of Cicero, Illinois, reaffirming the historic statements of the Christian faith as set forth in the Bible, God's Word, do regard the aforesaid action as having severed our fellowship with the Conferences and associations of the Congregational Church; and do hereby declare our connections terminated, and direct our Clerk to communicate this action to the State and local Associations, assuring them of our sincere regret that the circumstances mentioned above have made this protest and action necessary. BE IT FURTHER RESOLVED, that we as a church stand ready to associate ourselves with any group of congregations agreeing with us in the fundamental doctrines of the Word of God, who may feel led to take similar action, for the purpose of mutual helpfulness.

After time allowed for thorough discussion, the congregation adopted the resolution without a dissenting vote.

"From all you've said, Pastor, it seems to me that we're not the ones doing the separating," one man said in conclusion. "The denomination has already separated from God's Word."

"And I don't see how anyone can object to the spirit of this resolution. It states our views in a clear, but gracious way."

But what about our name?" another member worried. "It's still got the word *Congregational* in it. Do we want that?"

"Why not simply Cicero Bible Church?" came the answer. "*Cicero* identifies our place and *Bible* states our foundation."

Billy felt enormous relief that the decision had been made. The question of affiliation with another group remained to be decided, but in the meantime his daily scheduled activities kept him running.

The heart needs of his people were always his greatest concern. Hearing of a man who had visited the church and was in the hospital, he wrote:

> We are remembering you and your health and spiritual welfare in prayer. We are interested in you and your eternal welfare. If you have not definitely taken Christ as your Savior, let me urge you to do so. Do take John 3:16 and place yourself in it, thus making it your own.

Letters went out constantly, showing personal interest in those who accepted Christ in Sunday school classes.

> Your coming forward in our Sunday school on January 24 to confess that you had received Christ as your personal Savior brought great joy to your teacher and to myself as Pastor. We will be glad to help you in your Christian life at any time and in any way possible.

As he worked one day in his study at the church, the secretary knocked and opened the door.

"Pastor, a man is here. He says he must talk to you."

"A member?"

"I don't know him. He may have visited, though he didn't say so. He wouldn't give his name."

Billy waved a hand over his cluttered desk. "I'm pushed for time right now. Tell him — tell him to make an appointment. Work him in sometime tomorrow."

The secretary nodded and started to close the door.

"Wait!" Billy drummed his fingers on the desk a moment and then stood up. "Something is wrong with my schedule if I let it keep me from helping someone. Tell him to come in."

The secretary looked up when the study door opened an hour later and the man came out, shaking Billy's hand fervently, traces of tears still evident on his face.

When he left, Billy faced the secretary soberly. "I almost made a terrible mistake. The man was desperate, about to lose his wife and family because of drink. Now he's rejoicing in Christ. What if I had put him off until tomorrow?"

He went back to his desk with a fresh enthusiasm. But as he settled down and pulled papers toward him, he glanced at the clock. Almost three o'clock. The children would be coming home from school. Tonight was his Bible class in Racine. It would be a rush as always. He wouldn't see much of the children —

He got up impulsively, grabbing coat and hat. "I'm going home," he called over his shoulder. "Be in at the usual time tomorrow."

He strode along the street, scolding himself for the many times he pushed Minnie and the children to the fringe of his days. He took deep breaths of the crisp air. Just right for a quick game of touch football. The snow piled in the back yard would make it more fun.

The children shirked with delight when they saw him and trooped outdoors after him.

"Bill!" Minnie called from the back door. "Warn them about getting too close to the grape arbor. The branches are brittle, and a football will break them."

"Let's cut it down, then, so there'll be more room to play," he called back.

Minnie retreated to the house, a smile tugging her lips as she mixed a batch of cookies without the usual fingers reaching for licks of dough. How thoughtful Bill was to come just when she especially needed help with another baby on the way.

Myrtle came out to stand, watching her father, both of them thinking of the storm of tears in the argument she had lost with him the day before.

She leaned against the kitchen sink, her voice still sulky. "I'm the only one who never gets to do things. Why can't Dad see that I have different ideas than he does on some things?"

"Honey, I just can't believe that you are the only one

not allowed to go to movies. That's one of the standards of the church."

"That's just the parents' idea. Not all of us kids agree with it. And I'd sure like to wear lipstick once in a while."

Minnie bent to take a pan from the oven. "Well, you do," she answered calmly.

"You mean—you can tell?" Myrtle hastily wiped her lips with the back of her hand. "You didn't tell Dad?"

"He has eyes."

"How come he hasn't said anything?"

"He probably hasn't noticed." Minnie looked across the table at Myrtle, a faint smile curving her mouth. "I don't believe he has noticed either that you've cut your hair an inch or so at a time."

"Mother! I love you for not telling on me."

"Myrtle, I want you to know that I respect your father's stand. I have the same ideas he does—oh, perhaps not as strongly. And, of course, I see things from a woman's viewpoint. But just remember that Dad wants to guard all of you against the evils of the world. He wants you to be Christians who will stand for what you believe."

"Yeah, but right now we have to stand for what *Dad* believes. I mean, about not wearing lipstick and having short hair. It's hard for us kids to have to live by his standards."

"That's the price you pay for being William McCarrell's child. When you are older, you will appreciate your father more than you do now."

"You know I love Dad," Myrtle burst out. "It's just that he doesn't understand how I feel."

"You are fifteen years old, Myrtle—old enough to have some idea of the pressures your father is living with. He has the responsibility of the church and the big debt of the new building. There's the problem of the separation from the denomination. And think of the economic situation. It isn't easy to feed and clothe six children, four of them boys. And he wants all of you to have the advantage he didn't have of going to college. The times are a strain. Be understanding of him."

Chapter 8

The days following the church's final break with the denomination were so hectic with church needs that Billy had little time to plan for the next important step of affiliating with another group. He stopped to make urgent hospital calls on the way to the church office one day. Then he hurried to his study, knowing his desk would be piled with letters that demanded answers.

On top of the pile was one from the office of the president of Wheaton College. Tearing it open, Billy skimmed the brief lines.

"Glad to hear of the step you and your church have taken. Are you ready now to move ahead with another organization?"

He called to his secretary, "Get me all the correspondence on the American Conference of Undenominational Churches, please."

When the secretary brought the file, he rifled through it for the letter Dr. Buswell had written on June 13, 1927, shortly after he had become president of the college. The letter was terse, picking up on a previous conversation he and Dr. Buswell had had.

"I have been wondering why we do not get together

with our fellowship of orthodox churches. Let's move ahead."

Billy leaned back in his chair, lacing his fingers together as he stared out the window. He mentally reviewed the steps that had led him to break his church's connection with the denomination.

First had been his own strong opposition to the apostasy he saw engulfing seminary professors and ministers and reflected in church members. His opposition had grown stronger with every statement he heard that downgraded God and His Word.

Then Dr. Buswell's letter had come to encourage him that it was possible to survive as a church without a denominational connection. And, if his and other sound churches formed another, independent organization they would not only survive, but grow.

His eyes focused on the folder containing the many letters he had received from other ministers who were alarmed by the departure from the Bible by men in their denominations. He sorted through the letters and read again the one from a Presbyterian minister who had begged, "Tell us what we should do to make it impossible for our property to be taken from us in case we should separate from the Presbyterian body or a division should occur on account of doctrine."

Billy shook his head sorrowfully as he reread the letter. The lawyers he had consulted before answering the letter had said there was little a church *could* do.

The church property belonged to the denomination. To leave would mean losing the property.

Finally, last September had come the letter from a member of the American Conference of Undenominational Churches, suggesting that his church and others might want to join their conference. He looked at the copy of the letter he had written in reply.

> Overpressure of work has prevented a reply to yours of the fifth before today. Moving my study and church office, getting ready for Dedication Sunday and Week, getting the new building finished and furnished — as well as bringing up back work which accumulated while we were away for the summer — and having the ordination of four young men and getting three off to the mission field, has given us more than plenty to do.

He let the letter fall to the desk as he stared, unseeing, out the window. He thought of last fall and the enthusiasm over the new building that had infected everyone with confidence. Then had come the stock market crash, hitting so soon after he had written this letter. His sigh was almost a groan as he thought of the pressures on his people. Almost every family in the church had felt the drastic cut in employment. Some people were already living on the savings they had intended for old age.

People struggling to meet the essentials of shoes and food and rent couldn't be blamed for not having money for church light and heating bills. Yet, they *had* to meet payments on the church loan. They could not let the bank foreclose. The board and the congregation would have to make tough decisions soon.

The sound of his fist thumping the desk brought him out of his thoughts and back to the realities of the moment. He leafed through the correspondence again. He had told Minnie that the church could stand alone if it pulled out of the denomination. But he didn't want it to. There was strength in unity—the right kind of unity.

"We've got some hard battles ahead of us," he muttered. "It would be a wise step to unite with others who stand for the truth of God's Word."

He reached for the information he had about the ACUC. It had come from Mr. O. B. Bottorf, director of the St. Louis Gospel Center and newly elected president of the ACUC. The letter was candid.

> I was first contacted by the group from Conway, Arkansas, in 1927, asking if they could hold their 1928 convention with us at the Gospel Center. They sent along copies of their magazine, *The Pioneer of a New Era*. I was not impressed by what I read. The magazine showed how fuzzy the organization was on some essential doctrines. In fact, it was shot full of errors that I won't go into now. But there was warmth there and a love for the Lord. We here in

St. Louis have been burdened to form a fellowship of true-to-Christ believers who were forced from their denominations by apostate leaders. So we wanted to encourage these brothers.

Frankly, the mixture in that first convention made the prospects look pretty dim. But there was an earnestness and a warmth for God that lifted everything. Since then there's been a change of leadership in the group, and we've supplied some sound material for the magazine.

Last year's convention in Depue, Illinois, emphasized the need for a fellowship of fundamentalists. So, Brother McCarrell, hearing about the movement among the fundamental Congregational churches in the Chicago area to come out and be separate, we are asking you to join our group. We'd also like to hold our 1930 convention in your church if at all possible. I understand from a write-up in a Chicago paper, that you have a brand new building, which would give us plenty of room. Also, if we are meeting under your roof, it would help in clearing up any still fuzzy doctrinal matters.

Billy jumped up. This could be the answer. He strode to the study door. "Have you time to take a letter before lunch?"

Then, as the secretary picked up her notebook, he said, "No, wait. This is better handled face-to-face.

I'll arrange a meeting with Brother Bottorf and Dr. Buswell. I'm sure one of Minnie's good dinners will iron out any differences we might have."

He chuckled then and added, "That is, if we can suppress some of the children's pranks. The last time we had a guest, one of the boys rigged up a gadget under the table cloth at the guest's place. When he squeezed the bulb, the plate jumped. We all had a good laugh over it. But Minnie drew the line at the water glass that dribbled water down the chin when someone drank from it."

The secretary laughed. "Your six children certainly do make for a lively time."

The dinner meeting was successful. Billy shook hands with Mr. Bottorf before he left for St. Louis. His voice was rough with suppressed emotion as he said, "This could be the beginning of a mighty movement for God. The next step should be a meeting of anyone who is interested in joining us. We can air the whole matter — go over reasons why a church can legitimately pull out of its denomination. That will give everyone a chance to ask questions, state doubts, or give arguments for and against. How about holding the meeting at my church? Would you be able to come back for it?"

Mr. Bottorf nodded. "I'll be glad to attend. If I'm on the spot, I can answer questions about the movement and the magazine. Some men could legitimately question certain areas of the ACUC which are in error. But, of course, those are the areas we intend to change."

Coming back several days later for the meeting, Mr. Bottorf looked around the crowded room appreciatively. "You must have advertised well. Quite a group here."

"It shows how many men there are who want to transfer into a sound fellowship," Billy answered. "And these are just the men in this area. I'm sure there will be many across the country who will want to join us."

Then he urged, "Don't duck any questions that come up. Answer every one as fully as possible. If these men aren't satisfied that this fellowship will be different from their denominations, we'll lose them. They won't want to jump out of the frying pan into the fire."

The questions came thick and fast, probing and prodding, testing every aspect of the organization. At the end of the meeting, a unanimous vote to unite with the ACUC showed their eagerness to find a fellowship of men of like faith.

Mr. Bottorf took the floor again after the vote. "The next step is to have a convention to organize officially. It's February now. Can we plan one for May? Or perhaps June? And, Brother McCarrell, may we plan to meet here in your church?"

Billy nodded eagerly but said, "Let me present it to my people. As you know, we have already severed our relationship with the denomination. I am ready personally to join a movement that takes a stand against apostasy. And I believe my people have the same attitude. However, the decision must come from them."

When Billy presented the resolution to the church, the vote to unite with the ACUC was unanimous. Billy sent a telegram to Mr. Bottorf on February 26, 1930.

> At a well-attended meeting the church voted unanimously to join the American Conference on Undenominational Churches. The congregation also unanimously voted to extend an invitation to the conference to hold its June convention in this church. First Corinthians sixteen, verses thirteen and fourteen.

But Billy worried as he planned ahead to the June meeting. A small minority of the ACUC membership held unsound views and remained a problem to be faced. He laid out his fears in a long letter to Mr. Bottorf, who answered simply, "If God is in this, as I believe He is, He will take care of it all."

Busy as Billy was with plans for the June convention, they were only a part of the rush of his life. Invitations poured in, asking him to preach and hold meetings and teach Bible classes. Minnie waited up for him when he came home late and tired from meetings, listening as he poured out results and praying with him. He handed her a letter one day, his voice too husky from feeling to read it aloud.

"Mrs. Wilson's boy, thirteen years old, told me he has learned more about the Bible in the last six weeks [in a Bible class in LaGrange] than in all the rest of his life. He is so interested, he came early last week and helped me set up chairs. I'm so happy your exposition is so clear that a thirteen-year old is rejoicing."

This kind of encouragement made Billy eager to accept as many Bible teaching invitations as possible. An opportunity came from Kenosha, Wisconsin.

> If you feel that a series of meetings from Monday to Friday would be better than once a week for a length of time, we could fall in with your plans. We would, however, prefer one night a week for at least six weeks.

> If you come up on the North Shore train, you can leave Adams and Wabash at 6:05, eat on the train, and be in Kenosha at 7:20 in time to start the service at 7:30, as the church is only a five-minute walk from the depot. You can catch a train to Chicago at 9:42 which gets you to the Loop at 10:50. I trust you will be able to make a good connection with the El train to your home.

Accepting the Kenosha meetings added another evening to his already overflowing schedule.

He came home late from one meeting, unburdening himself to Minnie. "They asked so many questions about the gangsters that it was a depressing meeting. I tried to concentrate on the power of Christ to deliver anyone, no matter how sin-hardened he might be. I spoke of the thing that's always surprised us, Minnie, about the gangs. That is, that they have no compunction about bumping off a member who squealed to the police. They do it with the nonchalance of a man getting rid of rubbish. But those who have come to Christ for salvation are left alone. We've seen that here at Cicero. I pity those modernists who say there is no sin. I'd like to show them what some of these men have been saved from. Every one of them knows that only Christ could save him."

Billy attended the Sunday school Children's Day program in June and couldn't resist scribbling a list of practical suggestions for improving the next year's program. He jotted them on the back of an envelope.

1. The program was too long.

2. The parts should be announced (for the sake of strangers, boys and girls who can't read, and those without programs).

3. Adults questioning the graduates must speak up clearly.

4. Those taking part should face the audience. Make the welcome song louder.

5. Study the amount of time wasted in processionals.

This same attention to detail went into the plans for the important ACUC convention. Billy knew that careful planning with prayer was the key to success of any meeting. He drew up a convention sheet with detailed instructions for publicity; lined up ushers, a parking attendant, and a caretaker to arrange chairs and pick up papers and hymn books; and set up an information and literature table.

Because he was eager for his people to have as large a part in the conference as possible, he asked, "Would we be able to put up delegates in homes? The dates are June twenty-fourth to twenty-seventh, so they would be here three or four nights."

"Would the host family have to feed them?"

"Just breakfast. Each delegate could be charged — oh, perhaps a dollar for bed and breakfast."

"Oh, well, if the delegates pay something, that will help. A lot of the people could use that extra money. A dollar is mighty big these days. We won't have any trouble getting enough homes."

"Even for a hundred delegates? At least, I'm hoping for that many."

"Oh, yes." The board members nodded agreement. "We can care for them. The accommodations won't be as luxurious as at a hotel, but who could get a hotel room and breakfast for a dollar?"

When the delegates arrived and registered, Mr. Bottorf drew Billy aside, his face showing his relief. "The Lord has answered. The men we were concerned about have decided not to attend. We won't have to worry about the unsound element causing a problem."

"Good! But I wanted to warn you that I've picked up some rumblings, even complaints, about the name.

Do we have to retain the American Conference of Undenominational Churches?"

"No, not necessarily. Has another name been suggested?"

Billy nodded. "The one I've heard most often suggested is the Independent Fundamental Churches of America."

Mr. Bottorf frowned in thought. "We might have objections from some to the word *independent*. But it sounds good to me. All we are, after all, is a group of individuals and churches uniting in a stand against apostasy."

The convention days were filled with the hard job of stating objectives, explaining purposes, drawing up a constitution, and electing officers. Billy was elected chairman of the committee to draw up the constitution and the doctrinal platform. He rushed home between planning sessions to report the progress to Minnie.

He looked across at her as she sat mending, shifting in his chair. "I—uh—I wanted to tell you that I've been suggested as Executive Secretary of the organization."

"Bill! You won't accept, of course."

"Well—Actually, I've been elected already. But I wanted to tell you myself."

"But with all you have to do already, Bill! Taking on such a big responsibility will cut into your time for Bible classes—the Fishermen's Club—your mission preaching—your writing—the summer tent work— How will you manage?"

He leaned forward, his face and voice earnest. "Minnie, this organization could be one of the most important the world has ever seen. This fellowship of believers can be a—a refuge for men who are attacked in their denominations. Many men are ridiculed and even actively persecuted for believing the Bible. This organization may be a small step, but it is a step toward stemming the apostasy that is sweeping across the world. We can't completely defeat apostasy, but we can counteract it. We can at least slow its grasp on unsuspecting people."

He pounded he fist on the chair back. "I want to be part of it, Minnie, an active part. I want my voice to be heard. I want to be counted for Christ."

Chapter 9

He gave the same impassioned statement to the delegates when he returned to the church for the next meeting.

"Brethren, let us resolve that the Independent Fundamental Churches of America shall never be a denomination. Rather, let it be a fellowship of churches, Christian workers, and servants who are true to the fundamentals of the Christian faith. We want to be a fellowship of men who are endeavoring to stand for certain great truths which we believe are vital to Christ's cause. Let us determine that the Fellowship will ever be a haven of friendly encouragement to every Christian who is standing for biblical fundamentalism. Christ is the center of our faith. He is the all-sufficient One."

Billy waited for the hearty *amens* to quiet and then went on, leaning over the pulpit desk to punctuate his words with emphatic gestures.

"A Christ-honoring attack upon apostasy in every form is due our Lord, His Word, and His People—an attack that will awaken Christian to the eternal issues at stake. We must convict God's people of the sin of supporting apostasy through mistaken silence, cowardly compromise, or furthering apostasy by financial support of those churches that deny our Lord's incarnation, atonement, bodily resurrection, ascension, intercession, and return. Our Fellowship of Independent Fundamental Churches can lead the Christ-honoring attack."

A man stood up near the back of the room. "Mr. Chairman, can we define our terminology so that when we report back to our people they will understand what we are talking about. The word *apostasy*, for example, and *apostate*. Will you spell out exactly what we mean by those words?"

"Certainly. An apostate is one who at one time claimed to believe certain truths — in this case, truths about God and the Lord Jesus Christ — but has since repudiated those views. He may hold a position of leadership in his church or denomination and brazenly claim to be a Christian while denying God's Word and God's Son."

"So we're talking about separating from unbelievers *in* the church, not from those outside."

Someone else was on his feet, protesting, "No, from both."

"Wait a minute," shouted another delegate. "I don't like all this talk about separating. We're supposed to reach out to sinners, not cut ourselves off from them."

Billy pounded for order as a babble of voice swept the room.

"This is an important issue. Let's be sure we are all

clear in our thinking about the meaning of separation. We want to hold the view of separation that the Bible holds. It seems to me the Bible is clear that a believer is not to have fellowship with unbelievers — in the church or out of it."

"Fellowship is one thing. Reaching out to win them for Christ is something else," came a vigorous objection.

"Absolutely," Billy nodded. "But again, remember that we are defining an apostate as someone in the church who pretends to be a Christian but who denies the basic truths and doctrines of Scripture. God's Word charts a very clear course for every Christian to follow concerning separation from apostasy. God's methods in counteracting apostasy can never be bettered. Any endeavor to do so is sin. I would remind you of the command in God's authoritative and eternal Word in Second John nine through eleven.

> Whosoever transgresseth, and abideth not in the doctrine of Christ, hath not God. He that abideth in the doctrine of Christ, he hath both the Father and the Son. If there come any unto you, and bring not this doctrine, receive him not into your house, neither bid him God speed: for he that biddeth him God speed is partaker of his evil deeds.

"So what is our stand, Mr. Chairman? How do we state it?"

With everyone looking at him, Billy stood in thought. Finally he said, "I say that our position is biblical separation. First, from the apostate denominations and the ecumenical movements such as the Federal Council of Churches of Christ in America. Second, from such carnality and worldliness as is condemned in the Word of God. We want to be separated unto the gospel."

A delegate at the side of the room jumped up. "I say that we should refuse to fellowship with anyone who stays in an apostate denomination, even if he doesn't agree with what goes on in it."

A voice from near the back of the room asked, "So then, if I follow my conscience and pull out of my denomination—"

"You wouldn't just be following your conscience," the first man retorted. "You would be following God's command."

"Well, all right. But the point I'm making is that under the definition you've just given, if I pull out and, say, my son-in-law, or my parents, or my closest friends don't, then I can never have them over for Sunday dinner or whatever else is included in fellowship? Is that what you are saying? If so, I don't go along with it. I call that separating from a true believer, and I don't believe that is biblical separation."

"We're commanded to contend for the faith," said another delegate, his voice rising in anger. "It seems to me that anyone who chooses to stay in a liberal denomination is liberal, too."

"I don't agree." The quiet voice near the back

commanded attention. "I was raised in a liberal Presbyterian church. I was saved as a twelve-year-old because of the faithful teaching of a godly couple. They stayed in the church to serve, even though the liberal preaching grieved them. If they had pulled out, where would I be? There are many sound people in liberal churches. They stay because they have long-standing ties. They stay because they believe they can do some good. Brother McCarrell, what do you think?"

Billy nodded slowly. "You have a point. A host of great Christian servants in the past such as Riley, Gray, Chafer, Griffith, Thomas, and Scofield endeavored to stem apostasy by battling for Bible truth within denominational frameworks. Yet, despite their constructive, noble ministry, apostasy increased. Each year young Christians were told that apostasy would be corrected within denominations, but results have been the opposite. I believe the IFCA has come to the kingdom for such a time as this to encourage believers to come out of apostate denominations."

Men were on their feet all over the room, and Billy stood back, giving everyone an opportunity to speak.

Finally, he stepped to the front again. "I believe we are all in agreement that God's judgment rests on those men and churches who are apostate. Therefore, it seems clear that Bible-believing Christians cannot be connected with any such. We cannot honor men who do not honor God in their preaching. We cannot fellowship with—walk in agreement with, is what the word means—those who are not united in fellowship to God through Jesus Christ. The Lord commands His own to come out from among them. This means leaving those churches in denominations that make it clear by word and deed that they have turned from God."

"Brother McCarrell, of course I agree that we must leave churches that no longer adhere to the faith. But many churches within denominations are themselves sound. Some of them would lose their property if they pulled out. So they stay in, but preach the Word faithfully and give to missions—"

"Do they give money to missions through the denomination?" a delegate cut in swiftly.

"Well, yes. They do have certain obligations."

"I know a woman whose husband gave thirty thousand dollars to missions through his denomination just before he died. Now that money is sending out missionaries who preach good works instead of Christ crucified, risen, and coming again. His widow is heartbroken, but what can she do?"

"That's the reason believers must pull out of those churches. Money talks. If Bible-believing Christians withheld their money, the denomination would feel the pinch."

"But that would not solve the basic problem we're facing. Our policy should be to urge believers to leave the unsound denomination and *even* the sound church in an unsound denomination. Brother McCarrell, I believe that is the issue here."

Billy nodded. "I agree. Saved individuals who love God's Word but who stay in an apostate church are helping to build the apostate forces they claim to be against. Those are the forces that are undermining the Christian faith in the minds of the unwary."

He stopped, listened to a man speak in the front row, and laughed. "Our friend here has suggested that we have three options: We can sell out—which none of us intends to do—come out, or get kicked out."

After the laughter subsided, he went on. "Our main emphasis is not simply to fight apostasy, necessary as that is. In addition to fighting, we want to build constructively and be a bulwark against the liberalism we see flourishing on every hand. We stand first of all *for* the gospel of Jesus Christ, and then against those who oppose that gospel. Let's always remember that those of us who know the truth and believe it should stand for it."

A delegate stood, his voice choking as he spoke. "One of the greatest things about this organization as far as I'm concerned, is that, by joining it, my people, who are the only evangelical witness in our community, won't feel so isolated. At times we've thought we were Elijahs—the only ones left who stood for God. With this fellowship, we'll feel the pulse of others around the country who believe."

He stopped, folding and creasing the program in his hands, and then finished, "I'm — I'm a little ashamed to admit it, but I'm not as strong as Brother Billy to stand against criticism."

"Maybe you don't enjoy a good fight as much as he does," came a voice from the back of the room.

After the general laughter, Billy protested, "I don't think it is fighting to stand boldly for what one believes. Keep in mind that we must not squabble over secondary issues. But we can have a holy boldness, knowing we are separating from apostasy and in so doing we are obeying God's command. Remember, we are separating from those who deny Christ; we are not opposing fellow believers. However, we do want to encourage them to join us. We may have differences in church polity, but we must be united in our fundamental doctrinal stand. The importance of our separation cannot be emphasized too strongly. It will have a vital part in determining to what extent the present and future generations will enjoy Bible truth that saves, sanctifies, and glorifies."

"Mr. Chairman, when the committees meet to hammer out specific objectives, I think they must keep in mind that we want this organization to do two things. First, to provide a common ground of fellowship for any church or minister who has separated from a denomination that tolerates liberal preaching and teaching. Second, we want the organization to be an encouragement to *us* as we reach out with the gospel."

He sat down in the midst of clapping and shouts of "Amen!"

"This is what we all want," Billy responded. "The constitutional committee has a membership clause it would like to present. Let me read it to you."

> Individual ministers and Christian workers who can give assurance to the Credentials Committee of the IFCA that they are in hearty accord with the doctrines, aims, and purposes of this independent movement and are willing to obey the behests of the Spirit of the living God as He leads them forth into separation from denominational affiliation are eligible to membership.

"No, that's too wishy-washy," came vehement objections. "Only those who have counted the cost and have come out should be eligible."

"The committee feels that we must give time for men to respond to the light," Billy answered. "We may want to change the statement if we find it does not work after it has been fairly tested. But we believe this should be our policy now in these fledgling years."

"We probably will be changing the constitution in future years," another committee member reported. "But take careful note of the Preamble as you have it there before you. We believe it states our purpose very well."

WHEREAS, the large, established denominations, generally speaking, are now in the deadly grip of Modernism with its blighting and paralyzing influences; and, since prevailing conditions have caused many to withdraw therefrom, and to seek elsewhere the faith and fellowship most satisfying to their spiritual needs; in consequence of which, many independent groups of earnest Christians have been formed: and

WHEREAS, it has always been both an encouragement, and a more effective means whereby to prosecute the work of the Lord, for such ministers and congregations to join in a common bond of fellowship, counsel, and cooperation, so strengthening one another in the Lord's word; and

WHEREAS, in the providence of God, we believe the time has come for an advance movement among these independent churches and groups of Christians to thus unite in a closer fellowship and cooperation in the defense of the faith and in the proclamation of the gospel of God's grace:

WE DO THEREFORE, on this Twenty-sixth day of June, in the year of our Lord, 1930, form such a bond of fellowship and cooperation, as is set forth in the Constitution which follows, into which we heartily invite any and all churches and groups of believers, who share with us the same faith and doctrine.

"Please note, too," Billy added, "Article Three, stating our purpose."

> The object of this organization shall be to promote fellowship among God's people of like precious faith; to put forth every possible effort to disseminate the gospel; and to proclaim the whole counsel of God. This organization shall not only be thoroughly evangelical but it shall also be aggressively evangelistic.

Letters came immediately from pastors and churches wanting more information about the new organization. The word *independent* in the name bothered some. But the most serious objection came from those who feared the IFCA would in time become a denomination. A particularly strong letter came from a pastor acting as spokesman for others.

> The chief element of objection with all these people is the denominational aspect of the IFCA. All these men have been so cursed by it [denominationalism], that they are determined not to become narrowed by any such trappings in the future. There is the danger that the minute you admit churches as such into the organization, for all intents and purposes the movement becomes a denomination.

Billy's reply was quick and emphatic. "No! The organization's constitution states that it can never become a religious denomination. It is a fellowship of men and churches who desire earnestly to contend for the faith."

Chapter 10

During the long summer and bleak winter of 1930, Billy preached and visited and planned and encouraged his people as the depression deepened throughout the United States. Across the Atlantic gaunt figures began stumblingly to disappear into Stalin's frozen labor camps. Grim economic conditions in Germany prepared the way for the harshly strident voice of the man who was to bring terror and war and devastation to the world. Japan was at China's throat and invaded Manchuria.

But Americans during the 1930s had no time for or interest in anyone else's problems. Their own fight for survival was too grim.

Minnie concocted dishes to stretch meat to feed the seven hungry children. "Bill, what has *happened* to our country? Just a year or two ago everyone expected to be rich forever."

"My history teacher said the depression was caused by the European countries not paying what they owed us after the war," Myrtle said.

Gordon's voice was shaded with worry as he asked, "Is civilization going to collapse, Dad? One of my teachers said it would."

"God is in control of the world, even when men don't think He is," Billy answered. "Now is the time for Christians to put Second Chronicles seven fourteen into practice." He paused to look at the young, suddenly serious faces staring back at him. "It's a verse you children should know. Bill, get my Bible from the table and let's read it."

When Bill came back with it, he said, "Boy, Dad, you've got the most marked up Bible I've ever seen. I don't see how you can read some of the stuff you've written. The writing is so tiny. And this verse in Chronicles has got exclamation marks all around it."

"That's to show how important I think it is. Gordon, please read it."

> *If My people, which are called by My name, shall humble themselves, and pray, and seek My face, and turn from their wicked ways; then will I hear form heaven, and will forgive their sin, and will heal their land.*

Billy looked at the children. "Above all else, your mother and I continually pray that you will be godly men and women."

He took the children downtown as usual that Christmas to help them shop, rationing the quarters for gifts. He broke up a heated quarrel between two of the children.

"I want to buy Mama perfume, but *she* says Mama's rather have a paring knife or a cake pan." The son glowered at his sister.

Billy laughed. "It's true your mother might think perfume was a frivolous gift when she knows you don't have much money. But go ahead and buy her whatever you want to."

In April, 1931, he urged redoubled prayer by the congregation. "These are trying days for all of us, personally and as a church. You all know the bank crashed a few weeks ago, one of over two thousand that has closed so far this year across the country. We have over forty-six thousand there, including the fund for the new building. Only God knows if we will ever recover the money. But He *does* know, so we can be confident."

Billy met with his board in long sessions as they tried to see over the top of the burdensome debt.

"Men, these tight times are an opportunity for us to prove that God will provide for those who trust Him." He stopped and looked around the circle of faces. "That's why I'm suggesting that we go ahead with the project we've been talking about for the past months. Let's get that daily radio program started."

"Pastor! When we talked about that, we had money in the bank—people were working and had money to give. We knew we could swing it. But now—how will we pay for it?"

"We have some money designated for that purpose, enough for one month. If God wants us to continue after that, He'll provide the money as it is needed."

The men looked at one another, doubt clear on some

faces. Then the treasurer said, "I'm with Pastor Billy in this. Two contributions came in just this past week for the radio program."

The man next to him said, "Oh, well, if money is being given for it regularly, that's different. How much came in?"

"One gift was seventy-four cents, the other, twenty-six."

"Seventy-four cents! Twenty-six — how far will *that* go?"

"If you knew who sent those gifts, you'd know they represent a conviction that the radio program is an absolute necessity. That's why I say with Pastor Billy, let's go."

Billy spoke, quickly. "I've another suggestion — a conviction — one I believe God has given me. I'm convinced that the best answer to our financial problems is to give more to missions. Three young people have approached me in recent months about the possibility of our church supporting them in South America. I'd like us to recommend them to the missions board."

The board members were unanimous in agreement. When Billy reported it to Minnie she joined in thanking God for men with such vision.

But her dark eyes were sober as she asked, "Bill, can our church do something about the needs of the people right around us? At the school the other day, I was heartsick at the ragged clothes some of the children were wearing. And many of them look so thin."

"Could you get the women to organize a food and clothing relief project? Not just for the church family, but anyone who is truly needy. We can get a list from the city of those in the worst straits."

His enthusiasm brought paper and pen from his pocket as he planned. "We'll have to organize, and not leave the gathering of the food to a haphazard accumulation of whatever unused supplies people have in their pantries. We can start now to get food for the most needy cases and then build toward a broader Thanksgiving and Christmas distribution."

An appeal went to each Sunday school department. "Our Sunday school and church aims to help 160 families receive a splendid quantity of food during the holidays. The members of your class are given the opportunity to bring one five-pound sack of flour, or as many as they like, to the Christmas entertainment. Remember that Proverbs nineteen seventeen says, 'He that hath pity upon the poor lendeth unto the LORD; and that which he hath given will he pay him again.'"

Other classes were assigned other items of staples and canned goods with the reminder from 2 Corinthians 5:15 that "He died for all, that they which live should not henceforth live unto themselves, but unto him which died for them, and rose again."

When the food was brought, Billy reminded, "A definite witness for Christ goes with each gift, making clear that the greatest gift is salvation; the need for *it* is greater than any physical need."

His many visits through the years to preach in jails reminded him of the bleakness of prison walls. "So many of the inmates are forgotten men and women, never receiving a gift. Could we fill small boxes with fruit and candy and a gospel tract for each inmate in the city jail?"

"Would we have to get permission?"

"Probably. I'll contact the warden and see what restrictions he would have to put on us."

Billy laughed when he reported back. "The warden said he'd let in anything I was connected with. He said he knows me well enough to know there'll be no saws hidden in the boxes."

One of the men gave a wry smile as he said, "Some of us from Fishermen's Club were over holding meetings a couple of weeks ago. One of the inmates told us no one talked these days about breaking out of jail. He said they at least got fed regularly and had a warm place to sleep. That's more than some decent family men have."

Billy nodded soberly. "Times are getting worse, and there's no relief in sight. Some of those taking part in this project don't have much themselves. That's why I suggest keeping anything we do for the prisoners as simple as possible. Put an apple, an orange, a couple of cookies and candy bars, a small package of tissues, a tract, and a Christmas card with a Bible verse in a small box."

"Why not allow some leeway? Let people put in what they want."

"No, better to keep it uniform. That way they all get the same things, so no jealousies can start."

"How about including hospitals? There are a lot of lonely, forgotten people there, too."

Billy threw out his hands in an expansive gesture. "I hope this idea will spread to other churches. Ours can't begin to meet all the needs."

No one realized that Christmas of 1931 that the blackest days of the depression lay ahead. In 1932 twelve million Americans shuffled along the streets in worn-thin, cardboard-padded shoes, looking for work. By the end of the year one man in four was out of work, and so out of hope. Two hundred thousand American men, many in their early teens, left home to roam the country looking for jobs. Young teens, both boys and girls, were part of the horde of two million hoboes riding the rails, risking death from other vagrants or mangling by train wheels if they didn't hop on and off freight cars fast enough.

In Chicago, whole families picked through garbage cans, reminding Billy of the stories his father had told of past depressions. He and Minnie read the newspaper accounts of the 20,000 unemployed who paraded on Michigan Avenue, hoarsely begging for jobs. Men tried to support families by selling apples and pencils and shoelaces on street corners.

Minnie's voice quavered with tears as she repeated the story one of the children had told her. "Mark's father is a janitor in one of the schools. He can't afford the ten-cent streetcar fare to come home every day. So he has an army cot with a thin blanket in the furnace room of the school and cooks his meals on a one-burner hot plate; he only goes home on weekends. And then he often walks all the way to save the dime. Imagine! And his wife with the whole responsibility and worry of the family."

"If anyone can sympathize with her, it is you. You've had so much of the care of our children. I'm thankful some of them are old enough now to help."

After a moment he added, "I'm glad, too, that our bout with scarlet fever is over and the quarantine is lifted. I was telling someone the other day how the dining room looked like a hospital ward with the beds set up there for the sick children. And I was only allowed in the basement to keep the furnace going. Even with the church folks' kind help, I don't know how you managed those weeks."

But Minnie was still thinking about the newspaper stories. "Bill, I suppose the President is doing all he can, but nothing seems to help. Yesterday's paper had a picture of the shacks of tin and old boards people are living in. It's all they have. They're calling them 'Hoovervilles' in their anger at the President."

Billy sighed. "I'm afraid the whole depression is being blamed on him. And the soldiers' firing on the Bonus Expeditionary marchers in Washington has made people even more angry at him. I don't think he stands a chance of reelection. One good thing he's done is to go after Capone. He's been convicted of income tax evasion and sentenced to eleven years, probably in Alcatraz. Kind of ironic, isn't it? He made millions in illegal liquor, and money was his downfall. They couldn't seem to convict him for his greater crimes, like murder."

Minnie frowned. "It worries me that Roosevelt is in favor of repealing the Eighteenth Amendment, making liquor legal again. I know the amendment isn't observed as it should be, but how can they think conditions will be better if there is no law at all against liquor?"

"They claim that repeal will put a third of a million men back to work and give the government a billion dollars in taxes."

"They don't care about the broken homes and the heartache alcohol causes. And even women all over the country are organizing to support candidates who favor repeal."

"Well," Billy said, "not everyone is for repeal. There's to be a mass meeting at Moody Church just before the election. Dr. Ironside wrote asking me to attend and be listed as an honorary vice-president of the meeting."

"Will you?"

He shook his head. "No, Minnie, I told him I've ministered in Cicero, the heart of crime and illegal liquor, for over nineteen years, and have always adhered to a policy that kept the church apart from any political issues. A Christian has individual responsibilities in the matter of civic righteousness, but I believe the church as a church has no place. Of course I am for the Eighteenth Amendment, but it is not the church's work to put it over, nor to see that it is enforced. I told Dr. Ironside, I would tell people about the meeting and then leave it to them to attend or not."

"What was his reaction?"

"He was very gracious in his reply and agreed that the church should stand apart from all political issues. But he felt that Christian people should speak out for decency and righteousness. I agree, and we've been doing that here in Cicero all these years."

Billy tried to hold to his policy of not injecting politics into his messages. Yet his strong opinions on urgent political issues in the 1932 campaign showed strongly. In October a man in Grand Rapids wrote indignantly.

> I have been a member of your Bible class for several years and received a blessing for my soul. But now you have been trying to tell us whom to vote for. God has given us a mind to think and a weapon of prayer as well as you. He can reveal to us in His own way whom we should vote for. Several others do not care to go to the Bible class because you bring in politics.

Billy's answer characteristically began graciously, "I am so glad you attend the classes. Be sure to pray continually that I be kept in the center of God's will, and while in the center of God's will, that His words will be spoken through me. Surely this is my desire."

But then in defense he wrote:

> I have never felt that I bring politics into Bible teaching. The fact that I mention in an off-hand way, and often in a humorous way, something about the way I vote or the way I will not vote, is not exactly teaching politics. I have occupied this pulpit nearly twenty years, and have never given a political or patriotic sermon; and I never expect to. But I believe those in a popular audience must give a platform teacher a little leeway. Sometimes a remark is made with a little humor to pull back the attention of the class, and then different remarks are made for other reasons. For instance, I have often stated in my Grand Rapids class that I swung the last election for Hoover. I do not expect a person in the audience to take me seriously.

> Once in a while we mention things in politics or the current events because they fit into the Bible lesson as an illustration. I have no desire to dictate to the conscience of any person...I really feel that if any folks quit the Grand Rapids class because of the few trifling mentions I have made of the presidential election, they are using these trifling suggestions as an alibi. I am inclined to think that anyone who is really hungry for the Word and to grow in grace would see that any teaching upon politics was trifling indeed compared with the emphasis given God's Word and the Lord Jesus Christ.

Billy included a Scripture verse as always, in this case Hebrews 12:25–29, and ended, "Asking God's blessing through Christ upon you and your loved ones, and asking an interest in your intercession, I am yours and His through wondrous grace."

Billy's enthusiastic promotion of the IFCA filled his time not already claimed by the church and his weekly Bible classes. He was particularly touched by a conversation with Dr. Gray almost at the close of Dr. Gray's presidency of Moody Bible Institute. "The independent Bible movement is the nearest thing in church history along the lines of revival since the movement under the Wesleys. I am praying for you as president of the IFCA."

The burdens and pressures on Billy in connection with church needs, time given to furthering IFCA interests, and his many speaking opportunities were reflected in the many letters that came from his office. He wrote thousands of letters that were as full of Scripture as were his public and private conversations. He wrote letters of congratulation for birthdays, graduations, and anniversaries, letters of condolence, and letters of encouragement or exhortation. Even those written to correct showed the spirit of love. One closed, "I trust you will believe that this letter, though dictated in an effort to be frank, has been dictated in a spirit of Christian love and prayerfulness. Assuring you of our prayers for God's best through Christ on you and your work."

In 1933 he wrote a friend, "The Lord was good to us on our eastern trip, blessed the meetings, and brought us home safely. Because a church member drove us, I was able to take Mrs. McCarrell, Myrtle, Billy, and Ruth along. We saw many historical points."

But the same letter expressed his shock and dismay at a report that he demanded fifty dollars a week and his expenses for teaching in the mission in Grand Rapids.

> In the early part of my teaching last year I voluntarily reduced the amount they were giving me each week. In addition to this I gave small amounts to the mission out of that which they gave me. When the moratorium hit Michigan last year, I publicly announced to the class that I would receive the free will offering each Friday evening and out of that pay my traveling expenses and give everything over to missions. I did this every Friday night until the close of the class. Every Friday I announced what the offering was the week before, usually told my exact traveling expenses, and just what missionary work the balance went to. I have never set a price for a wedding, funeral, salary, Bible class, Bible conference, evangelistic meeting, or any phase of Christian work. By God's grace I never intend to. I always give all honorarium from weddings and funerals to missions.

He closed the letter with the plea, "I trust that you will do anything you can to correct the rumors that would reflect upon my personal testimony for Jesus Christ."

He shared his heartache with Minnie. Her eyes were shadowed with love and sympathy, remembering his long-ago promise to God that he would take any hard place with no thought of salary.

Chapter 11

With money the urgent need in everyone's mind, Billy began each day early in prayer and Bible study, seeking God's answer. He found a way to ease the financial burden of the church, but it was a method he had to discuss with Minnie first, before presenting it to the church.

"Could you manage if the church paid its bills first and then gave us our salary out of whatever money was left?"

"Of course. I've always managed on what you give me for household expenses. It's always been enough."

Billy's eyes were most with gratitude as he hugged her wordlessly. With his encouragement the church adopted a new financial policy in February 1934 to cope with the stringent financial crisis. Current bills were paid first from offerings and the remainder was pro-rated to the church staff. Everyone was eager to avoid adding any debt to the church beyond the building debt.

As Billy read of large denominational churches that were retrenching, cutting back on missions, eliminating programs, he felt a surge of exhilaration. Now was the time for believers to prove God, a time to show that God honored those who honored Him.

So his sermons rang with exhortation. "During these years of testing, when those in liberal churches are saying miracles do not happen, we have the privilege of proving God, of showing that He is the God of the miraculous. This depression is one of the signs of the times that God is working out His great plan for the earth. In these last hard years not one of our missionaries has had to wonder if his support money would come on time. Now is the time to advance, not retrench. Someone has suggested that the radio program could be temporarily stopped. But the radio reaches lonely people, desperate people. Listen to this letter which came in response to the Christian Businessmen's noonday message.

> I had tried everything… I had wealth… success. But everything in my life was falling apart. I decided the only way out was to take my life. I turned up the radio so the neighbors would not hear the shot. A voice—*your* voice, Rev. McCarrell—said, You've tried everything. Now try Jesus. He is the solution to every problem in life. That message saved me.

Billy and members of the board repeatedly appealed to each member to personally desire a closer walk with the Lord to counteract the insidious despair that cold and hunger and anxiety brought.

"Our aggressive, continual advance will defeat depression. We want everyone to know that God is still in the miracle-working business."

Billy stressed the joy and grace of giving in his sermons, speaking from Haggai and Corinthians. "The apostle Paul in Second Corinthians eight gives the secret of successful giving to the Lord's work. We must first give *ourselves* to Him. Then it will be no hardship to give from what He has given us."

The first Wednesday of each month became a day of prayer, beginning at seven in the morning with men stopping to pray on the way to work and others coming in throughout the day.

This foundation of prayer and trust in God gave church members incentive to find ingenious ways to save money for the offering. One member brought in two dollars to help pay the interest on the building debt. Knowing how little she had to live on, Billy asked, "How did you ever manage to save this?"

"Well, Pastor, I looked around to see what I was wasting, what I was carelessly throwing away. I looked for things that maybe could be used in some way. At first I couldn't think of a thing. Then I remembered the grocery bags I carefully folded and put away to use for garbage. I asked at my store what they would give for clean, neatly folded sacks. When I took back three hundred, they gave me this two dollars."

This sparked ideas in others' minds. They brought old pieces of jewelry to be sold for the gold and silver content. A careful accounting was given in each week's bulletin both of what was received and what the money was used for. The October 27, 1935 bulletin reported that $116.20 was realized from the articles brought in that week which included two gold tooth bridges, one earring, one gold bracelet, one gold pencil, two service pins, two 14-karat wedding rings, and one watch fob and chain.

The building debt weighed heavily on Billy and the people as a responsibility they had to meet. And, when met, it would be an evidence of God's blessing as well as a testimony to Him.

Billy searched Scripture for ways God's people had raised money for God's work and found an example in 2 Chronicles 24. "Joash wanted to repair the temple of the Lord and had a chest put at the entrance," Billy reported, excitement making his voice rise in volume and tempo.

"He asked the people to bring their contributions and put them in the chest. The result was that they gathered money in abundance. Can we try that idea? We've got a sample Joash box here," he said, holding one up. "Would each of you take home a box, either one for each family or one for each member of the family?"

He stopped, looking out at the eager faces, wanting to be sure everyone understood the purpose of the Joash box. "Just as in the account in Chronicles where the money was given willingly for the repairs of the temple, so the money in the Joash boxes is to be given willingly *for the building debt*."

He paused again to look around the quiet church. "That means what is put in the Joash boxes will be sacrificial, because it must be over and above what is needed for the regular work. We cannot, we must not sacrifice the missionary program. You have given so wonderfully through the years that our missions outreach has increased in spite of the depression. We thank God for that. But now the Joash boxes are for the completion of the building debt and this, for many of you, will be sacrificial giving. We will observe Joash Bank Night on December twenty-fourth, hoping to end 1935 with the year's payments met in full."

As they looked for ways to whittle down the building debt, the finance committee came up with another idea to enthusiastically bring to the congregation.

"When we began the project in 1927, the building cost two hundred twelve thousand," the finance committee chairman reported. "The balance now is one hundred thirty-five thousand. We ask prayerful attention to our effort to eliminate our last debt by pastor McCarrell's twenty-fifth anniversary in 1938. So we're asking you to buy building bricks at one dollar a brick. Every brick dollar will be used one hundred percent for the debt reduction. We hope many of you will take a number of bricks which can be paid for weekly, monthly, or yearly."

In spite of the pressures of money, the congregation had a surprise for Billy and Minnie as they planned for his twenty-third anniversary in 1936.

The man presiding built up to the surprise with a prepared speech. "Twenty-three years ago Pastor McCarrell delivered his first message in the little old Morton Park Congregational Church. The salvation of souls and the propagating of the Word of God has been the dominating policy throughout the twenty-three years. We unite in thanks and appreciation of Pastor McCarrell. Christ has been made more precious and His Word a living force as we have fellowshipped together in the Lord."

He stopped, grinned at Billy, and went on, "We want to give you something that will help in your ministry beyond the church. We all know how much time you spend riding trains in your traveling to and from speaking engagements. So, Pastor, we want you to have this car, because we know you'll use it for the Lord."

Billy was temporarily speechless and then had trouble controlling his voice as he thanked the people. But he added, "I'm afraid I'm too old to learn to drive."

"We've thought of that, too. We want you to call on any of us to drive you around until your boys are old enough to do it. Not that we think you are too old to learn," he added hastily. "We're just afraid you'll be so busy thinking out a message that you'll forget you are driving."

The laughter of the audience drowned out Billy's attempts at a reply.

Billy's many speaking opportunities meant that Minnie and the children frequently ate without him.

But when he was home, dinner conversations were lively. Sports was the most hotly discussed subject, with Billy's expertise often appealed to.

The long and loud conversations seemed longer on spring and summer evenings when the younger children gulped food and milk to get out to play before bedtime.

"Can I be excused, Mama?"

Minnie shook her head. "We haven't had our Bible reading yet."

"Daddy and Bill and Gordie are never going to quit talking," Ruth pouted. "They argued about that same game yesterday."

"And they probably will again the next time Dad is home," Minnie agreed with a laugh.

Billy tried to make up for the many evenings he was away by taking the children with him on trips to conferences. He always wrote them postcards and brought home gifts. The boys were crazy to learn to drive and willing to drive him to meetings when doing so didn't interfere with school.

Much of Billy's traveling and speaking was in his tireless promotion of IFCA, never begrudging the time and effort. He picked up on a suggestion that the IFCA initials could stand for I Find Christ Adequate, and used the slogan in his messages.

"The organization is still in its formative stage," he explained one day to a group of pastors who were asking about IFCA policy on ordination. "We have ordained some men, but we are reconsidering that policy. A special committee on ordination has been studying the problem. Their conclusion is that of all of the organizations in the country that should stand for things that are positive, definite, and scriptural in the men it ordains, IFCA is that organization. We will deserve the disgust of even our friends if our ordaining ideals are less than scriptural and our requirements of the men we ordain is less than respectable."

"But what is *your* opinion, Brother McCarrell?"

"Frankly, because of the difficulty I see of maintaining high standards, I personally am urging that the IFCA get out of the ordination business."

As Executive Secretary, Billy's office was flooded by letters either supporting or criticizing the fellowship. The initials IFCA were sometimes used derisively to mean I Fight Christian Anywhere by those who thought the organization was too separatist and divisive.

Some pastors who supported the basic principles of the fellowship were uncomfortable about the word *independent*. One man wrote:

> There are many true and honored fundamental pastors to whom the name "Independent" at once suggests a barrier to fellowship if they are not serving independent churches. They dismiss all thought of us until someone crosses their path who can give a detailed explanation. There is need of much explanation to show desirable prospects that the IFCA is a fellowship of ALL sound brethren

regardless of denominational affiliations. A number of true and greatly used fundamental pastors would find their ministry grievously and unnecessarily complicated if the become affiliated with a work labeled distinctly "Independent."

Billy replied, "Isn't Psalm thirty-seven a wonderful portion? Verse one, Fret Not. Verse three, Trust. Verse four, Delight. Verse five, Commit. Verse seven, Rest." Then he went on:

In my many years of experience I have found very few who mention certain weaknesses as a reason for not uniting with our organization who would unite even though we accept their suggestions. It is a growing question with me as to what extent our organization should encourage the membership of those who have not completely severed denominational connections. Should our organization become flooded with such men, its entire purpose might be thwarted. This question will have to be threshed out, possibly in the near future. And, it is my personal conviction that we should retain the word "Independent." Our organization was launched as an Independent movement. Independency has been one of our chief aims.

Billy found it necessary to write many such letters of explanation and reassurance. His enthusiasm for the IFCA spilled over into the pastoral classes he taught at Moody Bible Institute as he encouraged the male students to cut denominational ties.

He pushed a resolution formed at the 1936 IFCA convention, which declared its willingness to endorse any school whose program was in accord with IFCA standards.

"Young men going into the ministry need to be warned of the dangers of apostasy in denominations," Billy wrote and stated repeatedly. "Bible schools must include an essential course on how to establish, build, safeguard, and expand independent Bible works. Most Bible schools in teaching church history slight independent works."

Billy was particularly unhappy that Moody Bible Institute resisted the proposal, giving as its reason its position as an interdenominational school. But Billy never had time to brood about defeats or criticisms. When summer came, he plunged into the summer Bible school program and accepted invitations to speak at summer conferences.

"At least my conscience is clear that you and the children are having a good time at Cedar Lake," he said, as he helped Minnie pack after vacation Bible school was over.

She nodded. "We miss having you there, but we do have a good time. The children enjoy being outdoors from morning until night, and when it rains we play games. The Lord did a wonderful thing for us in making the cottage available to us for such a small price."

"The IFCA is planning to hold its first annual summer conference at Cedar Lake the week just before Labor Day."

"Well then, we might get a glimpse of you now and then between meetings," Minnie teased.

Billy threw back his head in a sudden laugh. "Someone asked me the other day if I was able to keep track of so many children."

"What did you say?"

"I just rattled off the names—Myrtle, Bill, Gordon, Jim, Paul, Ruth, Grace, David, and Danny—without stopping for breath. I think he was impressed."

As Billy planned his fall schedule, he answered an invitation to hold meetings by asking for prayer.

> I am having quite a struggle just now to ascertain the will of the Lord as to what I should do this fall. I am endeavoring to ascertain whether God would have me go out to different places a night at a time, or whether He would have me give my time to conducting Bible conference or special meetings in different towns from Monday through Friday, and then return to Cicero for the Sunday. I have so many invitations of this kind that sometimes it seems God is leading that way.

Billy came again and again to God for wisdom as he answered letters of criticism about men in the IFCA who were slow in severing denominational ties. To one such Billy wrote:

One gets the impression that you have already judged your brethren as to whether they will obey the Bible truth regarding complete separation. I find that many men do things because certain biblical light has not as yet gripped them. I prefer to at least give them a chance under the Word. Understanding and love is needed for men just coming out the denominations. Separation is an individual matter before the Lord, and some come to it slowly.

Other letters were easier to write, such as the one to a former teacher who had written him, "Willie, you were the last boy in the whole school I ever thought would be a preacher."

He replied:

When I review my life and think of the irrepressible and seemingly irresponsible and mischievous nature which was mine when I sat in your classroom, I now marvel at the grace and goodness of God toward me. It was a wonderful day when, in Pioneer Chapel in old South Harlem, I definitely placed my faith in the Lord Jesus. Thank you for your many kindnesses during boyhood days and for your encouraging interest in the years that have followed.

No matter where he traveled his heart remained in the church in Cicero. As the depression continued, he was encouraged that he did not stand alone in his efforts to resolve the building debt. The businessmen in the church and on the board continually wrestled with ideas to meet the enormous financial obligation the church staggered under.

"It's no comfort that other churches who expanded during the prosperous years are facing the same problems we are," one man sighed in gloom.

"It's the interest we have to pay on the loan that makes repaying the principal such a long process," another fretted. "We can't reduce the principal fast enough because of the interest. And not being able to sell the old building is keeping us in debt."

"Could we appeal to the members of the congregation to loan us money without interest?" Billy threw out the question tentatively.

"Who's got that kind of money to loan?" someone snorted.

"I'm not talking about big amounts. Even a twenty-five dollar loan would help—if there were enough of them."

"Hmm—it's *possible*—But what if someone loaned, say, a thousand dollars and suddenly had a emergency and needed it back? What would we do?"

"We would have to guarantee absolutely that those loaning money could have it back if needed," Billy answered promptly. "Of course, they would have to give us reasonable warning."

"You think people would respond to the idea?" came a doubtful question.

"Would you?" Billy demanded swiftly.

"Well—yes."

"Then let's call a congregational meeting and find out."

Billy prepared the proposal carefully so that everyone would understand exactly what was being asked of them.

"You know that we have tried various means of reducing our indebtedness. Yet, in a year we will be at the end of our ten-year mortgage with one hundred thousand left to pay. You have all given sacrificially out of your limited means. Now we are asking you for more. At the rate we are able to pay, we will be paying fifty thousand in interest. But if we all got together and loaned money without interest, we would be able to pay off the principal more quickly. Each one who loans money, regardless of the amount, will receive a first mortgage bond. If you have money in the banks, you're only getting one or one and a half percent interest, anyway. Loaning to the church interest-free means that we're giving to the Lord's work. Every penny loaned will go one hundred percent toward eliminating this burdensome debt.

The response was beyond what any of them expected with $60,000 loaned very quickly. Others in the community, intrigued by the idea, loaned $30,000. One woman bought church bonds and hurried home to tell her husband about the unusual opportunity.

"What?" he exploded. "You've thrown the money

I've worked for into that crazy scheme? Go get it back and I'll invest it in some safe place that will give us some return."

The woman explained the problem to Billy, her voice showing her embarrassment. He assured her he understood her dilemma.

"I think your husband is wrong in thinking your money isn't safe with us. It's not only safe now, but for eternity, too, since this is an investment in God's work. But, of course, we will return the money. We don't want to cause a division between you and your husband."

But Billy was curious and kept a check on the investment the man made. He heard later that the man lost his money when the investment failed, while the church honored every bond.

With such a diverse group constituting the membership of the IFCA, all of them men of strong convictions, Billy was frequently called on to smooth relationships. His reply often was, "I do trust and pray that the day will be hastened when all independent fundamentalists will be able to so witness, work, and stand together as to constitute a mighty force against sin, worldliness, and apostasy."

The squabbles and small bickerings suddenly seemed of little importance as he devoured the news during 1939. Stories filled the papers of scenes of frenzied people screaming "Heil Hitler" throughout Germany. There were pictures of Jews fleeing murderous mobs.

The hard boots of Nazi storm troopers thundered through cobblestone streets of one European city after another. Finally, the headlines were black with news of the outbreak of war in September 1939.

"We fought the war to end war scarcely twenty-five years ago!" Minnie's face was white as she stared at Billy. "Will we be able to stay out?"

He could only shake his head helplessly as he stared back at her, sharing her unspoken fear. *What will happen to our sons?*

Chapter 12

As 1939 ended, with much of Europe strangled by Hitler and Mussolini, anguish ate at Billy and Minnie, not only for their own sons but for the young men of the church as well. They read the papers and listened to news reports and wondered what the future held.

"There certainly is no sentiment for our country to get involved," Billy observed. "I hardly know what to answer people who ask my opinion. I don't want war, but I feel we do have to consider what obligation we owe those in the grip of totalitarian governments. Here we have President Roosevelt pleading with Hitler not to plunge the world into a war. And all Hitler and Mussolini do is heap scorn on him, knowing the general public in America does not want war."

In May and June of 1940 with the French army destroyed, swarms of German bombers and fighter planes flew over the English Channel trying to destroy the British Air Force. The British gathered their ragged resources and fought back under Churchill's defiant, "We shall fight on the beaches, we shall fight on the landing grounds, we shall fight in the fields and in the streets, we shall fight in the hill; we shall never surrender."[1]

And the isolationist mood in the United States began to change. In March 1941 Congress passed the Lend Lease Act, authorizing the President to sell, lease, or lend any commodity to any nation whose defense was essential to the safety of the United States.

"That means ships carrying those goods will have to be escorted by the American Navy," Billy said. "Some of them are bound to be sunk by German subs. I don't see how the President is going to avoid war."

His fears came true, and in early summer he came home to find Minnie wiping away tears after listening to somber news of the devastation in England. He put his arms around her to comfort her. "We've lived through this nightmare before and found God sufficient."

"Yes, but this time—" Her voice faltered. "This time—it will mean *our* boys—"

She stopped again, biting her lip and struggling to control her voice. "Bill, when I sat in the auditorium at Wheaton at commencement in June and saw you awarded the doctor of divinity degree, I was so proud of you. And thankful to God, because I knew how richly you deserved the honor. But mixed with it—inside—were tears as I looked at all the young men whose futures were so uncertain. And among them our own."

"I know. But we can pray that they, and the country, will be spared."

Billy tried to keep politics out of his messages,

but at times he related world events to Scripture. In September 1941, speaking on "World Chaos and God's Way Out," he warned, "The reason for the present world chaos revolves around Jesus Christ. The world has made a great mistake in rejecting the Son of God, for the events of the entire earth pivot around Him. No matter in what realm of life you look, you will find chaos—in government, in law enforcement, in finances. Today, we are in danger of seeing practically every invention of science dedicated to war. But after the nations have exhausted themselves, men will come to worship Christ. The first line of defense for the United States is not Britain or the mighty US Navy. It is the godliness in the hearts of the men, women, and children of this country."

War came in 1941, not from Germany but from a surprise bombing of the American fleet safely stationed in Pearl Harbor. Billy and Minnie listened in silence the evening of December 8 along with all Americans as President Roosevelt spoke of December 7, 1941 as "the day that will live in infamy."

The busyness of life had to go on, regardless of harsh world events. Myrtle and Bill had finished Wheaton College while Gordon and Jim were still students. They faced the prospect of the draft along with other young men from the church. "At least this time we're not hearing talk about this being a 'holy war,'" Billy commented to a group of fellow pastors.

As Billy traveled for the IFCA, he found a similar separatist organization emerging. The American Council of Christian Churches, formed in 1942, protested the Federal Council of Churches' claim that it represented all Protestants. The ACCC refused to allow as members any church that had any connection whatever with a denomination.

A number of IFCA men quickly and enthusiastically supported the militant stand of the new group and proposed affiliation.

"There is strength in numbers. We rejoice that others are following our example in taking an independent stand," they said as approval was voted.

Billy continued to face repeatedly the charge that the IFCA was a denomination. "No!" he exploded, as he had done the first time the fear was expressed.

Then, more quietly, he explained the IFCA position. "We do not ordain men to the ministry. Oh, it's true we did at first, but have not done so for a number of years. The IFCA cannot hold property. It does not raise missionary funds for distribution. It does not control the money, materials, or property of the local church. Each church adopts its own name and church procedures. Each year every individual member renews membership credentials and so reaffirms annually the doctrinal statement. The renewal of membership in our fellowship can be a great purger. Those who fail to renew their membership will automatically be removed form the roll. I want the organization to be easier to get out of than into."

One of the joint concerns of the IFCA and the ACCC was the small number of sound, fundamental chaplains in the armed service. The question was threshed out in the annual convention, and appeals were made to the government to allow IFCA men to be accepted as chaplains.

In response to criticism that the IFCA supported war, Billy declared, "We are not a pacifist organization. We believe that Christians should obey the government in time of war."

The war invaded their home with Paul's enlistment in the Army Air Corps in April 1943, when he was nineteen.

"I want to go in, Dad. If I do, I can get the training I want and maybe get out sooner. Helen and I are engaged, but we can't plan our lives until this is over."

"We have to let him go, Minnie," Billy said, trying to comfort her. "I'm afraid we'll see the other boys taken, too, before long. Just remember, no matter where they are, we've got them centered on Christ and in our prayers."

A few months later the church observed Billy's thirtieth anniversary as pastor. The article in the church paper exclaimed,

> [His] ministry has been an uncompromising testimony to salvation through personal faith in

Jesus Christ. Through his preaching many of us have learned of salvation. Through his consistent Christian life, many of us have been energized in our Christian lives. Through his efforts we have been able to grow up in a church true to the Word of God. In all these things we should give God the glory.

The church paper reported also the progress of the Building Fund. "Encouraging is the progress to date! Pray that this goal may be reached — $10,000 by December 26 — $30,000 as a tribute to 30 years of missionary ministry, Bible teaching, and evangelistic effort."

Billy encourage his young people now, as he had through the years, to attend Moody Bible Institute. He enjoyed the classes he taught, sometimes getting sidetracked on subjects of particular interest to him. One of those was the importance of Christians' being separated from the world.

"Let me give you young men some guiding principles I've learned from my own experience and the experience of others. First, avoid anything that hinders the best stewardship of time, life, and money. Avoid anything that would cause you to be misunderstood as a Christian. Avoid that which does not ultimately strengthen your spiritual life; do not be a stumbling block to others. Then, do nothing and be nowhere where you could not with joy meet the Lord Jesus. Finally, settle all matters with God's Word as the full and final authority."

A student raided his hand. "Dr. McCarrell, will you give us some pointers on how to get a church started?"

"I can tell you from experience that a branch work is a venture of faith. Our Lord's command to 'go into all the world and preach the gospel,' means to go where the people are. That is what branch works do."

"But what do you do first?"

"Find out which neighborhoods do not already have sound churches. I don't believe God wants us to go fishing in other people's ponds. There are plenty of places where there is no gospel witness. You find this out by house-to-house visitation, by phone calls, by use of the mails. The men in our Fishermen's Club are active in this."

"Then do you just announce that you are starting a church?"

"No. Usually you start in a small way with weekly Bible class, an evangelistic campaign, or a Sunday school. Careful organization has to follow, but don't organize too quickly. Build your membership cautiously and prayerfully. Work out a wise constitution. Adopt a biblical doctrinal statement and emphasize biblical evangelism. Exercise sanctified common sense in everything you do. Naturally, every step is done with prayer and the earnest seeking of God's will."

He chuckled as he looked at the intent faces. "You'll be surprised at the places that can be used. One of our branch works started in a pool hall, and a couple of others in garages. But then when you are ready to establish a permanent building, you'll have to clear a number of legal matters. Make sure of zoning ordinances; get a clear title to the property; and check local regulations for parking. Details like that can hinder a work if they are not properly cared for."

"Do you keep the branch work under your control? I don't mean *yours*," the questioner said hastily as Billy laughed. "I mean your church's control."

"We have what we call a 'Working Agreement' with our branch churches. The main purpose of the agreement is to make sure the branch work remains true to God's Word; that is has an orderly, well-run organization; and that the church gives us accurate reports of its progress. You see, we have also established what we call the Cicero Trust Fund. Members of the parent church loan money without interest to this fund which is then loaned to the branch work without interest. Eventually, the branch church repays the loan."

"Do they always stay branches?"

Billy shook his head. "That working agreement I spoke of has a preamble that says, 'When God so blesses the work of any branch of the Cicero Bible Church as to give evidence of its ability to function as an independent Bible church, that church stand ready to cooperate in launching said branch work as an independent Bible church.'"

"Dr. McCarrell, may I ask you something? How come you are so sold on independent churches?"

"Let me say one more thing about the value of branch churches that we've learned from the fifteen or so that we have established under God's leading. As you men go out into the ministry, you'll find that the closer a church is to its people, the more effective is its ministry. If you go where your people are in their daily lives of work and shopping and school, you will better know what their needs are."

Then he looked thoughtfully at the young man who had asked the question and repeated it: "Why am I for independent churches? Because they are one of God's most effective means of counteracting apostasy and stemming an overall decline in Christian work. They offer young men like you a challenging field of service. I've got a list of thirty-nine advantages of the independent church. I won't have time to give then to you today. But when any member of my church finds it necessary to settle in another church, I always advise them to refrain from uniting until they are certain it is true to God's Word—in pulpit message, Sunday school teaching, and methods of operation. I beg you young men to guard against a denomination that might not be true to the Word."

He looked at the serious faces, knowing some of the men were being called to military service. He and Minnie had already said good-bye to Paul who went overseas in December 1943. They wept with their church families who saw sons leave, fearing some of them might never return.

Billy sighed as he packed to leave for a speaking engagement. "Now that the boys are gone, I'll have to either take the train again or ask folks from church to drive me. Now I am too old to learn to drive."

Minnie leaned to put clean clothes in the suitcase and said casually, "If you let me know in time to make arrangements for things at home, I'll go along and drive."

She laughed as she looked at his speechless expression. "I've been taking lessons from that nice policeman's wife I've gotten acquainted with. I wanted to keep it a surprise for you. I haven't minded being home with the children all these years when they needed me. But now that even the youngest can be left, I am planning to go with you and be your driver."

"Minnie, after all these years you can still surprise me!"

The war years dragged by for everyone with several young men from ghe church killed in action, including Paul. Of the many difficult letters Billy wrote through the years, the hardest was one to his mother, dated March 9, 1945, telling of Paul's death.

> Minnie got the message as she was walking down the steps with the younger children for Sunday school. A government telegram stated that our dear

son was killed in action over Italy on February 17. He would have been twenty-two years of age on July 8. When the word came to me, I was in my study having just finished giving the radio message and preparing to go down to teach the adult Bible class. I went home at one. I will not try to describe the details, but everyone was strong by the grace of the Lord.

Jim left for overseas the day before Paul was killed. We have not been able to get any word to him. We sent Bill and Gordon wires that there was sad news and asked them to call home. It is hard to pray as a family, for as we go down name by name, we come to Paul—

However, we have been praying that God will memorialize Paul by using this to lead souls to Christ and to strengthen Christians in the Lord. We are surrounded by a host of friends, and God is using them to help us.

The heartache of Paul's death and burial with full military honors in a lonely grave in Italy, and the knowledge that Bill, Gordon, and Jim faced the same danger, kept Billy and Minnie seeking God's strength. Paul's loss was even harder to bear, coming just a few months before Germany's surrender in May. But at least the end of the war brought the other three boys home safely.

As Billy walked home from the office a warm spring day in 1947, the words of the letter he had just dictated repeated in his mind. "I will leave tomorrow for Akron, Ohio, come back for a few days, and then go to the Michigan Regional Conference on the next Monday near Detroit; back for one day and then leave for Minneapolis. These are busy days."

"I'm glad I'm busy, Minnie, in spite of the problems. And there are a lot of them. When you get a group of men together who have strong convictions, there are bound to be clashes of personalities. And, of course, the men in IFCA and the ACCC are men of strong convictions, or they wouldn't have dared take the stand they have. But sometimes it seems as though I spend too much time pouring oil on troubled waters. I wrote a long letter today and then felt I had to apologize to the man. I said how wonderful it will be when the Lord comes and we go into His presence. Then we'll be able to take 175 million years of a conversation and not have to be concerned about the time and strength element."

He looked at the clock and got up. "I must go. I have an appointment in Chicago."

"It's not as convenient for you since IFCA headquarters were moved from the church to downtown Chicago, is it?"

"No, but overall it's better. More central for making new contacts. I'm realizing more and more that we have to grow from newly established independent works, not just from men who leave denominations. The strengthening of our movement will mean much toward keeping the door of gospel proclamation open in public institutions, securing fair press publicity for Christianity, preserving gospel radio broadcasts, securing fundamental Christian Army, Navy, and civilian chaplains, and strengthening many other works vital to Christ's cause."

He stopped to grin at her. "You can tell that's a speech I'm rehearsing to give the other men this afternoon. Want to work it up into an article for the *Voice* also."

Letters came and went constantly from his office on IFCA business, and with regard to speaking engagements and writing he was asked to do for various publications. Sometimes the letters were needed to smooth hurt feelings. He wrote to a fellow IFCA pastor:

> I verily believe one of the weaknesses in our set-up is the tendency of some brethren to take up some technical point and carry it and roll it and roll it until they make it a burden for splendid overworked fellows like yourself...We have a stream of needless letters and conferences that don't amount to a hill of beans; to my mind, [this] whole thing wasn't important enough to justify moving a peanut half an inch.

Billy was caught in an exchange of letters concerning the publication of Sunday school lesson materials in the

Sunday School Times. The strong opinions of men in the ACCC caused a flurry of letters and resulted in hard feelings between some members of the groups involved. The editor of the paper wrote Billy, "Disagreements among conscientious Christian brethren are one of the most painful experiences of the Christian life."

And Billy answered characteristically, "Time, watered by prayer, often clarifies situations and heals problems."

His frequent first-hand experience with disagreements among his fellow pastors brought the earnest plea, "Let me assure you that it is my desire and determination by God's grace that present and future differences of position among true servants of God will not bring me to the place where I cannot love and pray for those whose course of action may be somewhat different from that which I follow."

He often turned with relief to the church, rejoicing in God's blessing. The church property was valued at more than $250,000, the membership rolls showed 1100 people with fourteen branch works successfully established. The daily radio program, begun with the widow's mite contributions, was seventeen years old and reaching thousands with God's good news. A letter to a friend in April 1947 rejoiced:

> God blessed the 24th annual meeting of our Cicero Fishermen's Club...The church is also purchasing time on two more radio station for our 11 P.M. broadcast, one in North Dakota and one in Texas.

Again we are now in possession of the large building to the north. God wondrously answered prayer and we were able to secure it for $55,000; no doubt it would cost $250,000 to build today. We are also launching out into the gospel sign ministry. The first sign, 25 x 55 feet with great gospel texts upon it, will be across from the Tribune Tower for one month, and be shifted about the city. God is good!

In 1948 the ACCC formed the International Council of Christian Churches and met in Amsterdam to "oppose liberalism and develop an evangelical world spirit."

Billy attended the international meeting as a representative of the IFCA, delighted that Minnie could go with him, and eager to see historic sites in Europe with her.

As they sat in deck chairs on the ship coming home, Minnie laughed softly. She answered his questioning look. "I was just thinking over the wonderful trip — the two days in Switzerland, the time in Paris." She laughed again. "Did I ever tell you what my boss said when I told him I was leaving my job to marry you?"

"If you did, I don't remember."

"He said he was sorry that I was marrying a preacher. He said I would never have a car or take any trips. And I've been sitting here going over in my mind all the good times the Lord has given me. Remember the 'honeymoon' escorted train trip the church folks gave us to Yellowstone Park the year before Ruth was born? And the 'Just Married' signs they put on our berths? And think of the places we've been together since I learned to drive. Now this trip to Europe. How little folks like my boss know how carefully God works all things for our good."

"Even Paul?" Billy asked gently.

"Even Paul. I've thought of him lying over here away from us. But, of course, he isn't here. I remember one line you wrote to your mother. 'Our immediate family circle is broken here, but it has begun in heaven.'"

1 Winston Churchill, "Speech on Dunkirk," given in the House of Commons, June 4, 1940.

Chapter 13

Billy came home from Europe to pick up his many responsibilities, including his writing ministry. He had written the Sunday school lesson outlines for the Union Gospel Press for many years. Now increasingly he was asked to write articles and editorials telling the origin and purpose of the IFCA. The requests came because "Some men coming in know nothing of the reasons for the IFCA. And many do not understand why there are other independent organizations."

So Billy wrote:

> When the fellowship was launched, one described it as the "shock troops of independent biblical fundamentalism." The prediction was made that it would be used of God to aid many Christians sound in biblical faith and desirous of constructive Christian life and ministry, to occupy a position of separation from apostasy. At that time apostasy characterized much of the life of major denominations and church federations. This sad condition has increased since that time. Those in the Independent Fundamental Churches of America should be encouraged by the fact that since the fellowship began, a number

of independent fundamental movements have developed. The attitude of the IFCA is one of friendship toward these fellowships.

In his relationship with others who held the same strong convictions he did about the necessity of separating from apostasy, he tried to maintain a balance of grace and truth and not squabble over secondary issues.

"It's best to hold Christian brethren together whenever possible. We may not always agree, but we should follow a policy not to unwisely criticize, embarrass, or attack an organization that is dedicated to Christ."

Billy was in demand as a speaker in regional IFCA meetings across the country, delighting in the fun of having Minnie along as his driver. In 1950 he went again as a representative to the ICCC convention in Europe, and this time went to Israel before coming home.

"How marvelous to see God working out all His promises," he reported back to his people. "How can anyone doubt God's Word when we see prophecy beginning to be fulfilled with the return of the Jews to their land. We do believe this must be the beginning of the end before Christ's bodily return to catch up His own."

The militancy of some other separatist groups began to increasingly disturb Billy and other IFCA men. Billy agreed with an article in the *Voice* that warned that such a militant attitude toward separation and condemnation of others could "Develop a ministry of denunciation, develop spiritual pride, and mistake separation from modernism for spirituality."

Billy nodded vigorously when he read the article and added, "I have often said that understanding and patience is needed for men coming in from denominations. We need to be patient with men who are fighting the same battle to separate that we fought. We have to live First Corinthians thirteen. The world must see that we love one another lest we make a mockery of our faith. The outside world, not aware of the issues involved, will see and hear only the bickering and in-fighting, and not understand the basic issues."

Finally a resolution was presented at the semi-annual meeting of the IFCA Executive Committee in December 1952 to consider severing connections with the ACCC; it passed at the annual meeting in 1953. But Billy and others were careful to restate the position IFCA had held from the beginning.

> Be it resolved further that the IFCA reaffirms without equivocation of any sort its historic testimony to complete separation from apostasy. We would remind all who may be concerned that as a fellowship of independent churches, the IFCA has been a pioneer in the matter of separation from apostate denominationalism. It is determined with God's help to continue and to strengthen

> its testimony is this direction. In so doing the
> IFCA will endeavor to follow the two Scriptural
> injunctions to "earnestly contend for the faith" and
> to "speak the truth in love."

At dinner one evening, Billy was so engrossed in thought that Minnie asked, "What problem are you turning over in your mind now? Another hard letter to write?"

He shook his head with a sigh. "No, I've been asked to write an article for the revised *New Schaff-Herzog Encyclopedia of Religious Knowledge* on the IFCA. My problem is I've got to keep it brief. They've only given me a few hundred words to tell IFCA's origin, membership, purpose, and organizational structure. I do have it roughed out. How does this part sound?"

> Membership is conditioned upon assurance of
> a desire to cooperate whole-heartedly with the
> fellowship's purpose and endeavor to oppose and
> counteract religious apostasy from Bible truth.

Minnie frowned in thought. "Will the people who read that know what apostasy is?"

"I'd like to spell it out, but it would take too many words. Anyway, then I thought of saying that a chief requirement is written assurance of belief, without reservation, in the doctrinal platform which is ultraorthodox in its adherence to every foundational phase of the historic Christian faith."

He stopped and looked back over his notes. "That's the heart of what should be said. I've tried to state it as clearly as possible in the few words allotted me. The rest of the article will be facts about the number of members, the magazine, and so on."

He looked across the table at Minnie, his eyes reflective. "Remember that tract Moody Institute put out so many years ago on the work here? They called it 'The Church That Did Not Close.' It was done, of course, as a promotional piece for the Institute, and I guess it did bring in quite a lot of money for the Institute's work."

"What made you think of it now?"

"I came across a copy of it in my files the other day. I was just thinking about the last paragraph. It said something about 'If someone were to write an Acts of the Apostles with modern chapters, surely the story of the church that did not close would be mentioned.'"

Billy stopped, lost in thought. Then he said slowly, "I've been thinking, Minnie. I'll be seventy years old next month. I'm wondering if it's time for me to let someone else take over the church."

He met her questioning eyes honestly. "No, I don't really *want* to leave. But—there are vexing situations from time to time that maybe someone else could better handle. And I want to get involved in other matters. If I could get rid of the heavy details of the pastorate, I'd have more time for Bible conference evangelism throughout the country and for lecturing in Bible schools."

Minnie watched him as he sat, musing out loud. "I want to write a number of books which will perpetuate my ministry after I'm gone."

"You already have a writing ministry, Bill. The Sunday school lessons you've written all these years, the tracts, the articles—"

"I know. But those have been done on the run. I'd like time to think through a book. And then, Minnie, there are so many other ideas I've had with no opportunity to work out the details."

He got up to pace in his excitement. "I've been dreaming of starting a Christian Work Center with a ministry of books and tracts and helps for pastors and laymen. I'd like to be able to solicit money to be channeled into independent Bible works. I'd like the opportunity to challenge young men in Bible schools to get into independent works. Then there are mission projects—one would be to encourage people to give money earmarked for a definite ministry such as opening a hospital or establishing an orphanage. There's so much I could do to help people catch a vision. But it takes time and thought to develop contacts."

He looked at her. "What do you think, Minnie? June of 1958 will complete forty-five years here. Shall we plan that way?"

"It's fine with me, Bill. But the decision must be yours

under God's leading. You and the church have been bound together for all your ministry."

After a moment she smiled and said, "I want us to plan something for next month. Let's go into Moody for the Founder's Week alumni day. It will be your forty-fourth anniversary of graduation, you know."

Billy felt a little lonely in the hectic rush of alumni day. He realized how few were left of those he had known as classmates. He eased his bulk into the hard wooden seats in the Moody Church auditorium, thinking of the years God had given him. He watched Dr. William Kuhnle, president of the Alumni Association, begin to present the Alumnus of the year award.

He came to with a jolt as Dr. Kuhnle said, "The alumnus we honor tonight is as old as the Institute, born the same month as Dwight L. Moody the founder, and the same year the Institute began, 1886."

Billy turned to look at Minnie, seeing the happy, proud smile on her face. They were talking about him!

Then he was escorted down the aisle and up to the platform with Minnie beside him. Dr. Kuhnle went on with the presentation.

> Dr. McCarrell graduated from the Moody Bible Institute in 1912 and the next year began his pastorate at what became the Cicero Bible Church. There were only a handful of people, and the church was ready to close its doors. But the young pastor preached with such zeal and testified with such

courage that before long the church began to grow. Now, after forty-three years, Dr. McCarrell is still pastor of the church. They have nine hundred in Sunday school and a congregation of over eleven hundred. The church supports thirty full-time missionaries and over the years many of their young people have come to study at MBI. Pastor and Mrs. McCarrell have eight living children.

This outstanding graduate has organized eighteen branch churches which are now self-supporting. He also organized the IFCA. He served on the faculty of the Institute from 1934 to 1952.

Applause lifted to the roof when Dr. Kuhnle stepped back to shake Billy's hand and motion him to the pulpit desk.

"It's a great honor to be named the alumnus of the year of the Moody Bible Institute," he began. Then faces stood out here and there, dear faces of his people, and he tried to smile at them.

"But I feel the honor also honors the people of my church and community. This happy occasion should pay tribute to a people who loyally and lovingly encouraged and labored with their pastor despite his unworthiness and weaknesses. We give God all the glory."

Chapter 14

Like Caleb in Joshua 14:11, who claimed, "I am as strong this day as I was in the day Moses sent me; as my strength was then, even so is my strength now," Billy's retirement years were crammed with activities. He summed up his schedule in a letter written just after his retirement.

"We are just getting settled after four months of Bible ministry in England, Scotland, and the north of Ireland. We were able to speak 102 times on the trip, get out over 20,000 tracts, and put about 3800 books into circulation. God richly blessed the Word. Much more could be said, but we are trying to catch up on accumulated work."

Then in 1965 he wrote a pastor who had asked him to come for a series of meetings.

An avalanche of work hit me just before a month of ministry in June in California. Since that time I have been busy getting ready to leave for Europe to speak at the Sixth Plenary Congress of the ICCC in Geneva, Switzerland. I had the task of preparing my address which had to be written up and sent on ahead so it could be translated into about four or five languages and printed up. When I return, I am scheduled for a week and two Sundays of meetings in the Altoona, Pennsylvania area.

This was a man of seventy-nine who was also busy with his Christian home for older retired people, speaking in Bible schools, attending the dedication of a men's dorm in his honor at the Appalachian Bible College, pastoring a church in Wisconsin, and traveling and speaking tirelessly for IFCA.

His death in August 1979 at ninety-three left a hole in many organizations. Through the years he had served on more than fifty organizations, boards, and councils in an administrative, advisory, or endorsement capacity. His association with the pacific Garden Mission covered sixty-four years from the days as a newly saved man he had rushed through Sunday dinner to teach a converts' class at the mission. He served at Wheaton College, much of the time on its Executive Committee. He was associated with Faith Theological Seminary, Bryan College, and the Chicago Hebrew Mission, was president of the Great Commission Prayer League and the Lightbearer's Association, and a teacher at Moody Bible Institute for eighteen years.

All this and more was in addition to establishing and building the Cicero Bible Church from a plant with no facilities and only a few members to a million-dollar structure with fifteen hundred active, growing, serving members.

Through all the years he remined true to the conviction God had given him early in his ministry—separation from apostasy in the church and worldliness without. Sometimes the emphasis on separation was a lonely stand. This was true in 1961 in connection with the Chicago Billy Graham campaign.

In spite of his personal appreciation of the evangelist's ministry, he said that his position was "trying to sell Brother Graham the idea of coming to Chicago with his own set-up and working with a committee of unquestioned evangelical caliber. I expressed the conviction that he might have the greatest campaign of his career in Chicago on that level. I did state that men such as myself who have built their entire ministry on the basis of separation from denominational apostasy could not toss their ministry over the fence in order to cooperate in a campaign which would use methods that would contradict everything they had stood for. I let it be known that if I cooperated on a level that violated such a separated stand, my own congregation would think I had backslid, and thousands who had followed me in separation from denominational apostasy would feel I had let them down."

Billy McCarrell has been characterized as a fighter. And he was—a fighter against sin. But he repeatedly emphasized, "From the beginning of my ministry, I have made it a habit never to step into a pulpit unless I could say to God that I love every Christian and am free from any wrong feeling toward anyone."

A letter to someone with whom he had had a sharp difference of opinion said, "My desk lamp has the following statement upon it: 'He that answereth a matter before he heareth it, it is folly and shame unto him' (Proverbs 18:13). In order to be consistent with the motto, I felt that I should write to you directly."

In assessing life, one cannot wholly depend on a man's judgment of himself. Billy McCarrell was seen from a variety of perspectives.

His church said: "Through prosperity and in depression, through one world war and now another, Pastor McCarrell has continued to hold forth the gospel of the Lord Jesus Christ as the only answer to the need of mankind. What cause, then, has this people to be grateful to God for our pastor, who has in all things given Christ the preeminence!"

A long-time member of his church reminisced, "Brother McCarrell had a deep dedication to the Lord and to personal witnessing. People loved his Bible Classes. His usual method was to start with Genesis and go right through the whole Bible. He loved the Word. He never had any problem finding sermon material because he loved the Scripture. He could be strict and demanding. I have heard him angry about apostasy. But he was at his best when his heart was mellow—when he was deeply moved and concerned about people. He had a delightful sense of humor. He was patient and loving to people who were backsliders. His sincere love for the Lord, for people, and for the Word made him appreciated by the derelicts of South State Street as well as the trustees of Wheaton College."

Another man wrote, "He is a man of one book, the Bible, chiefly self-trained in the school of everyday service, and known for his uncompromising stand for separation from the world in message and church methods."

A missionary wrote to the church:

> I think there is no living man who did more for me that Dr. McCarrell. Both my wife and I were brought to the knowledge of Christ under his ministry. We were taught to love the Word of God, we were encouraged to pray, to fill out hearts with the Bible, to witness to others, and further, that having been saved, our lives were no longer our own, but belonged to God. I praise God upon every remembrance of that quiet, powerful, outstanding man of God.

> I was present when Wheaton College bestowed the honor of Doctor of Divinity upon him. I inwardly wept with emotion as I saw this man so honored, placed in high ranks of recognized men of spiritual accomplishment. I well remember how I thought how it will be when God bestows rewards and honors upon him and others of like faith and faithfulness. In the Wheaton Chapel all were quiet

and respectful and solemn at the time of his being honored. I thought of the quietness of multitudes in heaven that will be his when God crowns him with His special honors of faithfulness to His divine call and responsibilities.

Billy frequently quoted the advice he had been given early in his Christian life. "While a young Christian and before my life plans were formulated, a preacher from Scotland told us one day that it would be heaven on earth for a Christian to live in the center of God's will. He also warned in his blunt way that it would be hell on earth *not* to live in the center of God's will. I have found that living in the center of God's will is not easy, but it is necessary."

Minnie lived with Billy in the center of God's will and found it not easy, but necessary. "I had a husband who loved me and his children, but he loved the Lord also and put Him first in his life. The Lord gave us our love for one another, and because of His great love and mercy, it lasted almost sixty-five years."

The opening sentence in a biography of a queen of England said that if she were not a queen, no one would write a book about her. The reason for a book about Billy McCarrell is that he served the God of glory for seventy-five of his ninety-three years. He entered his Lord's presence on August 25, 1979, to receive the crown of faithfulness.

Other books by William McCarrell

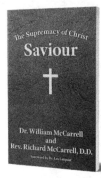

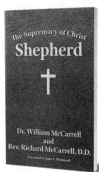

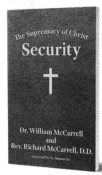

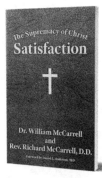

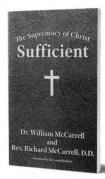

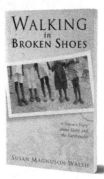

9 781602 650602